Sexuality and Translation in World Politics

EDITED BY

CAROLINE COTTET AND MANUELA LAVINAS PICQ

E-INTERNATIONAL
RELATIONS
PUBLISHING

E-International Relations
www.E-IR.info
Bristol, England
2019

ISBN 978-1-910814-46-8

Production: Michael Tang
Cover Image: Aldo Soligno

A catalogue record for this book is available from the British Library.

E-IR Edited Collections

Series Editors: Stephen McGlinchey, Marianna Karakoulaki & Agnieszka Pikulicka-Wilczewska
Books Editor: Cameran Clayton
Editorial assistance: Benjamin Cherry-Smith, Assad Asil Companioni, Tomek Najdyhor, Anjasi Shah and Alexander Stoffel

E-IR's Edited Collections are open access scholarly books presented in a format that preferences brevity and accessibility while retaining academic conventions. Each book is available in print and digital versions, and is published under a Creative Commons license. As E-International Relations is committed to open access in the fullest sense, free electronic versions of all of our books, including this one, are available on our website.

Find out more at: http://www.e-ir.info/publications

About the E-International Relations website

E-International Relations (www.E-IR.info) is the world's leading open access website for students and scholars of international politics, reaching over 3 million readers annually. Our daily publications feature expert articles, reviews and interviews – as well as student learning resources. The website is run by a registered non-profit organisation based in Bristol, UK and staffed with an all-volunteer team of students and scholars.

Abstract

When terms such as LGBT and queer cross borders they evolve and adjust to different political thinking. Queer became *kvir* in Kyrgyzstan and *cuir* in Ecuador, neither of which hold the English meaning. Translation is about crossing borders, but some languages travel more than others. Sexualities are usually translated from the core to the periphery, imposing Western LGBT identities onto the rest of the world. Many sexual identities are not translatable into English, and markers of modernity override native terminologies. All this matters beyond words. Translating sexuality in world politics forces us to confront issues of emancipation, colonisation, and sovereignty, in which global frameworks are locally embraced and/or resisted. Translating sexualities is a political act entangled in power politics, imperialism and foreign intervention. This book explores the entanglements of sex and tongue in international relations from Kyrgyzstan to Nepal, Japan to Tajikistan, Kurdistan to Amazonia.

Caroline Cottet is a co-founder and field coordinator of the Refugee Women's Centre, a charity that operates in refugee camps in Northern France. She is also editor-at-large for E-International Relations. Her activism and research focus on gender, migration, and militarism.

Manuela Lavinas Picq is Professor of International Relations at Universidad San Francisco de Quito (USFQ) and Loewenstein Fellow at Amherst College. She contributes to international media outlets and has held research positions at Freie Universität (2015), the Institute for Advanced Study (2013), and the Woodrow Wilson Centre (2005). Her latest book is *Vernacular Sovereignties: Indigenous Women Challenging World Politics* (University of Arizona Press 2018).

Contents

INTRODUCTION
Manuela L. Picq and Caroline Cottet   1

1. THE NAMELESSNESS OF LIVES: WHAT'S NOT IN A NAME?
    Cai Wilkinson   13

2. JAPANESE 'LGBT BOOM' DISCOURSE AND ITS DISCONTENTS
    Ioana Fotache   27

3. TRANSLATING 'QUEER' INTO (KYRGYZSTANI) RUSSIAN
    Mohira Suyarkulova   42

4. INDIGENOUS SEXUALITIES: RESISTING CONQUEST AND
    TRANSLATION
    Manuela L. Picq and Josi Tikuna   57

5. DOING SEX RIGHT IN NEPAL: ACTIVIST LANGUAGE AND SEXED/
    GENDERED EXPECTATIONS
    Lisa Caviglia   72

6. ASEXUALITY, THE INTERNET, AND THE CHANGING LEXICON OF
    SEXUALITY
    Jo Teut   85

7. BETWEEN EMANCIPATION AND OPPRESSION: THE BODIES OF
    KURDISH LIBERATION
    An interview with Diako Yazdani, by Manuela L. Picq   95

8. DECOLONISING QUEER BANGLADESH: NEOLIBERALISM AGAINST
    LGBTQ+ EMANCIPATION
    Ibtisam Ahmed   101

9. DONORS' LGBT SUPPORT IN TAJIKISTAN: PROMOTING DIVERSITY
    OR PROVOKING VIOLENCE?
    Karolina Kluczewska   112

10. THE COMMODIFIED QUEER SUBLIME
    Soheil Asefi   127

GLOSSARY   135

NOTE ON INDEXING   138

Contributors

Ibtisam Ahmed is a Doctoral Researcher at the School of Politics and IR at the University of Nottingham. His research is a decolonial killjoy which critically evaluates the toxic ways that British colonialism conceptualised itself as a utopian civilising mission, with the aim of shifting the focus towards anti-colonial and local narratives.

Soheil Asefi is a journalist and scholar. He studied Political Science at The New School for Social Research and is a PhD student of Sociology at the University of Nevada. Soheil Asefi was Nuremberg's guest under the German PEN project "Writers in Exile", and received the German Hermann Kasten award. He has written on the politics of belonging, commodification, imperialism and the dimensions of democratisation and neoliberalisation in the Middle East.

Laura Bensoussan attended the École de Condé (Paris) for a preparatory year in fine arts, and the ESA Saint-Luc (Brussels) for a degree in illustration. She specialises in children's books, having most recently published *Jeu Dans l'Espace* (Feuille de Lignes, 2018), with two other books forthcoming in 2019.

Lisa Caviglia (BSc Medical Biochemistry; MSc International Health; PhD Anthropology) researches gender and sexuality, and transnational migration between Asia and Europe. These topics have been addressed in recent media and scholarly publications, including "Sex Work in Nepal: the Making and Unmaking of Category" (Routledge, 2018) and "Outsourcing Love" (Economic and Political Weekly, 2017). She is currently focusing on "Traditions of Yoga and Meditation" at the School of Oriental and African Studies (London, UK).

Ioana Fotache is currently pursuing their Ph.D in Socio-cultural Change Studies at Nagoya University. Their research is concerned with LGBTQ+ activist narratives in Japan, and the way in which queer people negotiate their personal, social, and political identities on a personal, local, and global level.

Karolina Kluczewska is a post-doctoral research fellow at the research centre CERAL, University of Paris 13. She holds a PhD in International Relations from the University of St. Andrews. Karolina has research and practical experience in the development sector in Tajikistan, including collaborations with civil society organisations, international organisations and local academic institutions.

Mohira Suyarkulova is an Associate Professor in the Department of Sociology at the American University of Central Asia. She received her PhD in International Relations from the University of St Andrews in 2011 and since then has held teaching and research positions at universities in the UK, Germany, and Kyrgyzstan. Her research interests include the politics of modernisation and development, gender and sexuality, environmental politics, nationalism, and statehood and sovereignty in Central Asia.

Jo Teut (they/them/their) serves as Assistant Director of Diversity and Inclusion Programming at Centre College after serving as Diversity Specialist for the University of Wisconsin Extension and, now defunct, Colleges. They received a MA in Women's, Gender, and Sexuality Studies from the University of Cincinnati. They presented on asexuality at the National Women's Studies Conference, North American Asexuality Conference, and Creating Change Conference and created educational programming on asexuality for the University of Cincinnati LGBTQ Center, NASPA: Student Affairs Adminis-trators in Higher Education, and multiple queer conferences.

Josi Tikuna (Josiane Otaviano Guilherme), is a researcher in anthropology who graduated from the Institute of Nature and Culture at the Federal University of Amazonas, Brazil. She coordinates the Project Agrovida-Naãne Arü Mãü and collaborates with Brazil's Indian National Foundation (FUNAI-CRA-AS). As an active member of the Indigenous movement, she has presided over the indigenous students' commission at the Ministry of Education and Culture. She is the author of various articles on Tikuna queer sexualities.

Cai Wilkinson is Associate Professor in International Relations in the School of Humanities and Social Sciences at Deakin University in Melbourne, Australia. Her research focuses on how gender and sexuality shape experiences, perceptions, and articulations of security. Cai is currently working on projects about the politics of LGBT human rights and "traditional values" in the post-Soviet space. Her work has been published in journals including *Security Dialogue*, *Journal of Human Rights*, and *Critical Studies on Security*.

Diako Yazdani is a Kurdish-Iranian filmmaker who currently lives in Paris, France, as a political refugee. *Kojin* (2019), his first feature film, discusses homosexuality and homophobia in the Kurdistan of Iraq today.

Introduction

Sex, Tongue, and International Relations

MANUELA L. PICQ AND CAROLINE COTTET

The word 'queer' is not translatable in Spanish, so Ecuadorians say *cuir*, translating queerness into a term of their own (Falconí 2014; Falconí, Castellanos, and Viteri 2013). There are plenty of LGBT politics in Japan, but the Japanese language has no letter 'L'.[1] How do LGBT politics function without the L? What are the implications of translating a political movement into a language that does not have the words to say it? The politics of sexuality are radically transformed during the process of translation, be it in Ecuador or Japan. Language allows us to make sense of things, ourselves, and the universe we inhabit. Yet, time and again, our selves are lost, displaced, and reinvented in the process of translation. Gayatri Spivak (1993) concluded that translation is, in every possible sense, necessary but impossible, and Jacques Derrida agreed that what must be translated of that which is translatable can only be untranslatable (2001, 258).

Translation is about crossing borders. The word's etymology means 'to take across'. Sexualities evolve as they cross borders, they change while moving and settling anew. They resonate differently in different surroundings because translation is a process of constructing meaning. Once on the move, the language of sexuality is uncontrollable. Sexual terms, policies, and instruments can never be fully controlled by their senders; they are constantly altered in the processes of translation (Berger and Esguerra 2018). Translation is therefore a political act, an act of transgression, subversion, and appropriation.

Some things are untranslatable. The untranslatability of words refers to a space beyond naming, raising the question of what is visible and accessible. It points to the limits of turning life into words, calls for nameless lives beyond

---

[1]   Ioana Fotache, this book.

genders.[2] The untranslatable is that which escapes dictionaries, archives, and official history. It refers to a form of belonging that cannot be named or transferred, only experienced. The official histories of nation-states are translatable; the rebellions of subjugated people against domination are not. Histories of resistance are untranslatable worlds repeatedly left off the map. They are inscribed in intangible forms of being that lie on the other side of Empire (Carcelén-Estrada 2016).

Language tends to cross borders in specific directions, and some languages cross more borders than others. Spivak (1983) argued that subaltern voices cannot speak, that they do not exist and therefore cannot be translated. The subaltern cannot be translated because they cannot even start to come into being. The same is valid for sexualities. If subaltern sexualities cannot speak, they cannot come into being through translation.

Translation is also about betrayal. It is impossible to translate without some degree of epistemological (and ontological) captures of other practices and worlds. This is why the subaltern cannot speak, because their worlds are automatically effaced once translated into English. In a way, the voices in this volume are working to 'betray' the English language with its 'modern', Western LGBT frameworks.

Flows of sexual translation are anything but random. Translation happens usually from dominant to dominated languages, from hegemonic centres to subaltern peripheries – not from the periphery to the core. Translation as a transfer of knowledge is never equal. When we discuss the translation of sexualities, we do not mean translating Bengali, Nepali, or Kurdish sexual references into English. Instead, the translation of Western LGBT sexualities onto the rest of the world is usually implied. Translating sexuality in world politics forces us to confront issues of emancipation and colonisation, intervention and sovereignty, in which global narratives are locally embraced and/or resisted. Translating sexualities from the core to the periphery is a political act entangled in power politics, as well as histories of imperialism and foreign intervention. This is what this book focuses on: the entanglements of sex and tongue in international relations.

Knowing and the Anglosphere

The way we speak shapes the way we think. And the way we speak International Relations (IR) is in English. IR has long been described as an American social science (Hoffman 1977) that is not so international (Wæver

---

[2] Cai Wilkinson, this book.

1998), doomed for its US-centrism and knowledge production limited to the Anglosphere.[3]

IR scholarship is overwhelmingly written in English for English-speaking audiences. The top three IR journals are located in the US (*International Organization, International Studies Quarterly, International Security*), and US-based authors account for 80% to 100% of articles published in any given year between 1970 and 2005 (Friedrichs and Wæver in Tickner and Wæver 2009). This trend extends beyond IR. Almost 60% of the total literature covered by the Social Sciences Citation Index is authored or co-authored by scholars affiliated with the United States; all of Western Europe accounts for 25%, Latin America 1%, and the entire African continent for less than 1% (Keim 2008 in Tickner 2013). The construction of knowledge in the social sciences is by and large a business of the global North, in academic-refereed journals edited in English. These patterns of knowledge production are embedded in power dynamics that shape intellectual dependency. Scholars in the rest of the world have no option but to use terms defined in (by, and usually for) the Anglosphere. This limits not only the authorship but the substance of the study of the discipline (Bilgin 2016).

The Anglosphere therefore shapes the way we make sense of world politics. The fact that most IR knowledge is limited to English means that all forms of knowing the world in other tongues are almost automatically excluded. To echo Robert Cox's take on theory, IR theory is made by the Anglosphere, from the Anglosphere, for the Anglosphere. This inevitably silences our ways of knowing non-English sexualities.

This book resonates with a growing discontent among IR scholars. More and more scholars are exploring how to do IR differently, expanding disciplinary boundaries to include other ways of being in the world. Critics contest the pervasive ethnocentrism of theories that trace their genealogies to Hobbes and Locke but never to Nehru or Quijano (Blaney and Tickner 2017a). They accuse the discipline of being provincial and complicit in relations of domination, of not being all that worldly and trapped in the prison of colonial modernity. Scholars engage with questions of difference, non-Western thought, and ontological challenges to broaden the theoretical horizon of the discipline beyond its single-reality doctrine (Acharya 2014; Blaney and Tickner 2017b; Shilliam 2011). While there is a vibrant literature on queer international relations, attention to issues of translation is still marginal and epistemic dominance all too prevalent to learn from alternative worlds (Weber 2016; Rao 2018). This edited volume seeks to fill that gap, engaging frontally

---

[3]   Anglosphere is a collective term for English-speaking nations that are rooted in British culture and history.

the challenge of translating global sexualities.

Traveling Terminologies

A book on sexualities requires a note on terminology. The global sexuality framework is largely associated with LGBT politics, an acronym that refers to L(esbian) G(ay) B(isexual), T(ransgender). This short code can be expanded to various degrees, assembling a host of sympathetic allies up to the umbrella acronym of 'LGBTTIQQ2SA' (Lesbian, Gay, Bisexual, Transsexual, Transgender, Intersex, Queer, Questioning, Two-spirited and Allies'). The most common umbrella term is 'LGBT', although it has reductionist problems. As editors, we embrace and engage with all non-conforming sexualities, named and unnamed, and leave it up to the contributing authors to determine language in their own terms. Our intent is to recognise the fluidity and diversity of lived experiences, their untranslatability, and to reflect on the implications of translating sexuality politics across borders.

We recognise inherent tensions between the fixed codification of LGBT acronyms and the intrinsic fluidity of queerness. While LGBT politics categorise sexualities in the positivist terms designed to advocate for legal rights, queer approaches open an excess of possibilities to resignify sexualities, even the monolithic LGBT categorisation. The queer is inherently transgressive, challenging the determinism of LGBT identity politics, and may be a privileged space for translanguage.

Sexual vocabularies evolve among linguistic frames, gaining new meaning and changing interlocutors as they adjust to the context. Leap and Boellstorff (2004) explore the articulations of same-sex desire, what they call 'gay language', in the face of globalisation across cultures. If there are sexual cultures, they say, there must be sexual languages (Leap and Boellstorff 2004, 12). The book pays special attention to English, but contests the notion that cultural contexts influenced by global forces necessarily become more like the West. Instead, they describe the ways in which people renegotiate forms of gay language into different conditions, reworking global same-sex dialects into the local.

Every border is a reminder that sexual languages do not travel well, neither across space nor time. With all its intrinsic fluidity, for instance, 'queer' is a word that only exists in English. It is a word doomed to travel fixated in its English form. Latin Americans went *cuir,* making it speak to their own local realities in an experience of *trastocar,* letting words act as territories and become sites for theory.[4] These border crossings raise epistemological challenges that become political ones. How can we achieve international understandings of sexualities that are enclosed within a politically situated language? Is English the *lingua franca* of sexuality? Is the term 'queer' trapped in a neocolonial matrix? (Falconí 2013). The dialogue with other languages is vital, yet sexuality politics are embedded in global sexuality frameworks that are lost in translation.

Complexities range from epistemological issues about the value of assigning fixed labels, such as gender or sexual orientation, to the fact that LGBT categories are neither universally recognised, as many cultures do not subscribe to these Western identity-based concepts, nor do they capture the full range of sexual diversity. Translation can be the opportunity to undo a global term for local appropriation, both reversing established knowledge and defining new ways of belonging beyond the state-defined terms.

On Translating Sexual Politics Across Time

The terms LGBT, homosexual, gay, lesbian or queer have now become part of day-to-day language across the core-periphery divide. Not just in countries like the United States and the United Kingdom: these words and their variations can be found in China, Brazil, Spain, Russia, and Sudan. In Mandarin Chinese, for example, the most commonly used word for lesbian nowadays is 拉拉 (pronounced 'lā lā') which is directly derived from the English term. In visual representations, the rainbow colours are all over Chinese LGBT groups, both online and offline. This influence is relatively recent. Rich historical elements form a 3,000 year-long timeline of various same-sex sexualities and affinities, with a panoply of different social and political meanings, in (what now corresponds to) Chinese culture. Yet the direct and indirect presence of English language and culture around gender and sexual identities, which arrived in Chinese cities in the late nineteenth century and has fuelled activist organising since the 1990s (especially in Beijing and Shanghai), has had an influence that is now hugely visible.[5] This relationship between the two cultures and languages is anything but linear, and the consequences of this relationship are manifold.

---

[4]   Trastocar as an act, brings the Spanish prefix for reverse (*tras-*) in reaction with the image of *tocar* (touch) that can refer to affect, as in the act of impacting and changing through different levels of affection (Picq and Viteri 2016).

[5]   A rich research on the history of male same-sex practices in China has been carried out and published by historian and linguist Bret Hinsch (1992). On more recent developments since the 1990s, Yujie Guo who is a local activist, central to the movement, has written on this topic for E-IR (2015).

This historical development is not unique to China. Sexuality and the politics linked to sexuality have become increasingly global since the turn of the twenty-first century, as has been argued by Dennis Altman (2001). The contemporary promotion of these words and their usage on a global scale has primarily grown out of the Anglosphere and more specifically the Anglo-American context, sometimes vaguely termed *Western*. That the English language has been influencing, or rather dominating, other languages around the world is of course not limited to sexuality or gender. While it is the case in popular culture and scholarship, it is also evident in politics and economy. English has long been the language of power, and it dis/em/powers the way we speak/think/do gender and sexuality around the world.

All this matters beyond words. The language used in the present reflects a certain reality of the past and defines the possibilities of the future. On a personal level, gender and sexuality are components of the very core of how people define and understand themselves. The words people choose to express themselves carry a lot of meaning and connotations, depending on the contexts in which they are used and received. In South Africa, for instance, there are people who go by the name *sangoma*. *Sangomas* are traditional healers who are women with dominant male ancestral spirits, and who choose women lovers. Can they be labelled 'transgendered', 'lesbian', or even 'bisexual'? These terms would erode the complexity of *sangomas*, and the interconnection between their sexuality, gender, and spirituality. In many spaces, ideas and identities around sexuality didn't exist in the same ways as those included under the LGBTQ umbrella, and so the merging of cultures leads to a variety of outcomes, as portrayed in this edited collection.

On national and transnational levels, the language around sexuality has had legal, political and economic repercussions. Most visibly, Pride celebrations in June each year, and national debates around same-sex relationships and marital status have global resonances. In less obvious manners, the recent Anglophone connotation of LBGTQ culture has been used as a basis for many state leaders to actively oppose same-sex relationships, despite the existence of various practices all over the world long before colonialism. This was the case with Robert Mugabe in Zimbabwe, who, at several occasions during his time in power, called homosexuality 'un-African' and a 'white disease'. Yahya Jammeh of The Gambia and Yoweri Museveni of Uganda are also examples (Evaristo 2014; Bosia 2014). In contrast, there are many instances where the LGBTQ movement has enabled the rallying of people under a common banner, for the promotion and defence of individual rights. This was the specific reason for its creation at the Stonewall Riots in the first place. It has enabled the inclusion of lesbian, gay, and bisexual people in the United Nations definition of a refugee since 1999 – thus making it explicitly possible to apply for and be granted asylum on that basis (Miles 2010, 5).

Conversely, it also limits, in an Anglocentric manner, the categories of sexuality which are accepted as the alternatives to heterosexuality. So the consequences are complex, and the experiences uneven.

Emancipation or oppression? What if emancipation reproduces other forms of subjugation? The contributions in this volume reveal how processes of translation are entangled in layers of self-determination. Which experiences are translated with which words? From where? By whom? The chapters tackle the problem of sexual liberation to show how global narratives assert the existence of diverse sexualities but also impose external arrangements.

Overview of the Chapters

This edited volume explores sexuality from an interdisciplinary approach that crosses linguistic, political, and methodological borders. Multiple voices inside and outside academia reframe understandings of sexual languages across the world. Authors tackle the implications of translating sexualities from Kyrgyzstan to Nepal, Japan to Tajikistan, Kurdistan to Amazonia. They explore the impossibilities of translation, the value of unnaming and the importance of articulating a/sexuality in words. Authors engage Bengali and indigenous experiences to trace the lasting colonial rule over sexualities. They engage different methodologies in complementary ways, weave scholarship with photographic interventions and a comic strip. Here, poetry complements historical analysis, and memoirs resonate with activism. Within the multiplicity of approaches, all chapters share a common concern with the language of emancipation. The contributions explore what words liberate and what rights restrain, suggesting that the expansion of global sexualities is a tricky endeavour that can both liberate and oppress.

The opening chapter on nameless lives sets the tone for the book. Cai Wilkinson wonders what a nameless life would be like. The essay contemplates the notion of namelessness as emancipatory, providing momentary relief from the friction of ill-fitting words and potential permission to stop trying to explain oneself. It tackles the naming of sexualities as a politics of recognition, analysing the giving of (gender) names, the claiming of names to assert one's existence, the changing of names that function like maps, the undoing of names that alter reality, and the emancipatory potential of namelessness. Naming can be empowering, yet it also contains, codifying non-normativity as the new norm.

Ioana Fotache analyses Japan's 'LGBT Boom' and its position within national and global queer discourse. The essay shows how queer history evolved in the Japanese national context facing different obstacles and developing its own terminologies and performances until the 'LGBT Boom' of the 1990s, when local referents switched to anglicised terms and symbols. Queer advocates have chosen to keep the L in LGBT, and engaging in vernacular activism with anglicised references.

Mohira Suyarkulova discusses the impossibilities of translating 'queer' into Kyrgyzstani Russian. The author explores the role of translation which becomes itself a metaphor for queerness: forever oscillating between binaries (fidelity/infidelity, source/copy, original/interpretation), making the familiar strange and complicated, and revealing the contingent nature of language. The author compares two translations of *Queer Nation Manifesto* to show competing interpretations of the 'queer' in the post-Soviet space. LGBT and feminist activists in Kyrgyzstan have embraced *kvir* as a practice of resistance, a concept still confusing for many within the community/ies. Queer, it is argued, will continue to be translated in multiple ways. There can be no one 'correct' translation.

A comic strip by Laura Bensoussan talks directly to the lived experiences of homoaffectivity in Tikuna communities of the Brazilian Amazon. The comic strip illustrates the persecution of two Tikuna women as they are forced to flee their home chased at gunpoint by family members. This visual rendition speaks to the chapter on indigenous sexualities co-authored by Manuela Picq and Josi Tikuna. They take a linguistic approach to show that sexual diversity has historically been the norm, not the exception, among Indigenous peoples. Indigenous queerness, in its own contextual realities, predates the global LGBT framework. Yet Indigenous sexualities are lost in translation. It is not their idioms that are untranslatable as much as the cultural and political fabric they represent. Indigenous sexualities defy contemporary LGBTQ frameworks. The problem is not only that the global sexual rights regime cannot account for the place of desire in pre-colonial societies, but that discussing Indigenous sexualities in English runs the permanent risk of anachronism and misrepresentation. Indigenous sexualities are embedded in the impossibilities of epistemological translation.

Lisa Caviglia tackles the language of rights for alternative genders and sexualities in Nepal. An ethnography of transgender experiences in Kathmandu reveals the complex implications of sexual rights language. Nepal's sexual landscape has seen significant progress in terms of legal and social recognition. Identity documents now mention the category 'O' for 'other' in passports and *tesro lingi* in national identity cards. The author argues that if the international language of LGBT rights provides a sense of self and justice, these categorisations also create the expectation of conformity to non-conformity, impeding lives to oscillate between two different worlds. The author shows how the language of rights creates boundaries around identities that are otherwise more fluidly practised. Nepal's *tesro lingi* should not be reduced to 'transgender' but instead understood as 'third space', and the best expression of Nepalese pliability in the performance of gender and sexuality.

The lexicon of sexuality expands to asexuality with Jo Teut. The author explains the struggle for the recognition of asexuality with the development of new language, how it is pushing queer theorists to reexamine their own assumptions, their theorisation of desire and attraction, and what it means to be queer. The author insists on the valuable expertise of members of the asexual community to resist narratives that try to cure or fix. Further, the author analyses the material importance of having the language to articulate experiences and to resist imposed definitions, notably from disciplines like psychology. Teut surveys the depth of language the asexual community has created for itself, how language can evolve to match experience, new ways of delineating desire, and the linguistic potential of asexuality for informing queer theory.

An interview with Kurdish director Diako Yazdani brings cinema's language to the forefront. His documentary film *Kojin* tackles homosexuality in Iraq's Kurdistan, exploring the texture of queer lives in a society that fights for territorial freedom but resists sexual emancipation. For Yazdani, emancipation relates to the body. The film shows the limits of liberation struggles that deny homo/sexual emancipation. 'There can be no real solidarity among Kurdish peoples if we remain hostages to homophobia, if we are still controlling each other's bodies'. Everyone defends freedom, but freedoms translate into different practices for different people. The discussion tackles the importance of translating scholarship into oppressed languages, so that peoples under occupation are able to participate in global debates on sexuality produced and circulated in hegemonic languages.

Ibtisam Ahmed also connects struggles for emancipation with sexuality. The author shows the flaws of neoliberal LGBT approaches in Bangladesh, making a point for active queer decolonisation in the South Asian context. The chapter analyses the creation and uses of Section 377, a legal tool that framed un-English sexual behaviour as uncivilised, in conjunction with the Criminal Tribes Act to police queer identities, showing how empires weaponised gender and sexuality. The chapter reclaims Bengali histories of queerness suppressed through colonialism to critique LGBTQ+ liberation as a form of neo(liberal)-colonialism. The focus on Bengali queer struggles shows the flaws of reducing hijras to the global trans struggle, which failed to protect queer lives in Bangladesh. While international solidarity is important and Western allies can provide much-needed security, it is argued that activism itself must be grounded in decolonisation.

Karolina Kluczewska questions the impact of international support to LGBT people in Tajikistan. The text opens with a quote from 55-year Umed who misses Soviet times. A historical overview of LGBT issues from Soviet times to the present shows how Tajikistan became a battlefield for LGBT rights, with a significant backlash against the foreign promotion of LGBT norms. Interviews with key leaders tackle perceptions of right and wrong sexualities, social arrangements that separate private and public spaces, and growing tensions between tradition and Westernisation in the context of a nationalism perceived in opposition to Western individualism. Yet there are few options. While it is easy to criticise the activities and approaches of the donors' community, it is more difficult to offer alternatives.

The book closes with a political memoir which questions the commodification of sexual identity politics. Soheil Asefi narrates America's commodified queer sublime from a ferry tour to Staten Island with his mother, both survivors of Iran's political prisons. From the ferry, itself a symbol of crossing, the author tries to connect the dots and the intersection between queerness, freedom, and the creation of self. Asefi takes us from the sublime embodied in ordinary travellers on the ferry, to the solitary confinement of Iranian prisons to the commodification of LGBTQIA liberal venues. We are forced to question belonging in a system that successfully exported the politics of 'coming out' and the 'visibility' package across borders without reaching beyond identity politics. Weaving memories with theoretical debates, the chapter invites the reader to see how normative and non-normative genders and sexualities sustain international formations of power.

References

Acharya, Amitav. "Global International Relations (IR) and Regional Worlds." *International Studies Quarterly*, 58, no. 2 (2014): 647–659.

Altman, Dennis. *Global Sex*, Chicago, IL: University of Chicago Press, 2001.

Berger, Tobias, and Alejandro Esguerra. "Introduction: The Objects of Translation." In *World Politics in Translation: Power, Relationality and Difference in Global Cooperation*, 1–21. London: Routledge, 2018.

Bilgin, Pinar. "'Contrapuntal Reading' as a Method, an Ethos, and a Metaphor for Global IR." *International Studies Review*, 18, no. 1, February 19, 2016, 1–13. Bilkent University.

Blaney, David L., and Arlene B. Tickner(a). "Worlding, Ontological Politics and the Possibility of a Decolonial IR." *Millennium* 45, no. 3 (June 2017): 293–311.

Blaney, David L., and Arlene B. Tickner(b). "International Relations in the Prison of Colonial Modernity." *International Relations* 31, no. 1 (March 2017): 71–75.

Boellstorff, Tom, and William L. Leap. "Introduction: Globalization and "New" Articulations of Same-Sex Desire." In *Speaking In Queer Tongues: Globalization and Gay Language*, 1–21. Urbana, Illinois: University of Illinois Press, 2004.

Bosia, Michael J. "Museveni's "Gay Peril" in Global Perspective." Critical Investigations into Humanitarianism in Africa (blog), May 29, 2014.

Carcelén-Estrada, Antonia. "Oral Literature." In *Routledge Handbook of Literary Translation*, edited by Kelly Washbourne and Ben Van Wyke. New York, New York: Routledge, 2018.

Carcelén-Estrada, Antonia. "Response to Vicente Rafael: Betraying Empire: Translation and the Ideology of Conquest." *Translation Studies* 8, no. 3 (July 2015): 1–5.

Derrida, Jacques, and Lawrence Venuti. "What Is a "Relevant" Translation?" *Critical Inquiry,* 27, no. 2 (2001): 174–200.

Evaristo, Bernadine. "The Idea That African Homosexuality Was a Colonial Import Is a Myth." *The Guardian*, March 4, 2014.

Guo, Yujie. "It's Time for China's Lesbians to Speak for Themselves.*" E-International Relations*, August 18, 2015.

Hinsch, Bret. *Passions of the Cut Sleeve: The Male Homosexual Tradition in China*, Berkeley and Los Angeles: CA: University of California Press, 1992.

Hoffmann, Stanley. "An American Social Science: International Relations." *Daedalus,* 106, no. 3 (1977): 41–60.

Leap, William and Tom Boellstorff. *Speaking in queer tongues: Globalization and Gay Language*. University of Illinois Press, 2004.

Miles, Nathanael. *No Going Back: Lesbian and Gay People and the Asylum System*. Report. London: Stonewall, 2010.

Rao, Rahul. "The State of 'Queer IR'." *GLQ: A Journal of Lesbian and Gay Studies*, 24, no. 1 (January 2018), pp. 139-149.

Shilliam, Robbie, ed. *International Relations and Non-Western Thought: Imperialism, Colonialism and Investigations of Global Modernity*. New York, New York: Routledge, 2011.

Spivak, Gayatri Chakravorty. "The Politics of Translation." In *Outside in the Teaching Machine*, 179–200. New York, New York: Routledge, 1993.

Spivak, Gayatri C. "Can the Subaltern Speak?" In *Marxism and the Interpretation of Culture*, edited by Cary Nelson and Lawrence Grossberg, 271–313. Urbana: University of Illinois Press, 1988.

Tickner, Arlene B. "Core, Periphery and (Neo)Imperialist International Relations." *European Journal of International Relations* 19, no. 3 (September 2013): 627–46.

Tickner, Arlene B., and Ole Wæver, eds. *International Relations Scholarship Around the World (Worlding Beyond the West)*. 1st ed. London: Routledge, 2009.

Trávez, Diego Falconí. "Resentir Lo Queer/cuir/cuy(r) En Ecuador." *El Telégrafo*, March 24, 2014.

Trávez, Diego Falconí, Santiago Castellanos, and María Amelia Viteri. *Resentir Lo Queer En America Latina: Dialogos Desde/con El Sur*. Barcelona: Egales, 2013.

Viteri, María Amelia, and Manuela Lavinas Picq, eds. *Queering Paradigms V*, (Bern, Switzerland: Peter Lang UK, 2015) https://doi.org/10.3726/978-3-0353-0768-9.

Wæver, Ole. "The Sociology of a Not So International Discipline: American and European Developments in International Relations." *International Organization* 52, no. 4 (1998): 687–727.

Weber, Cynthia. *Queer International Relations*. Duke University Press, 2016.

1

The Namelessness of Lives: What's Not in a Name?

CAI WILKINSON

An Encounter and a Thought

Poem

I lived in the first century of world wars.
Most mornings I would be more or less insane.
The newspapers would arrive with their careless stories,
The news would pour out of various devices
Interrupted by attempts to sell products to the unseen.
I would call my friends on other devices;
They would be more or less mad for similar reasons.
Slowly I would get pen and paper,
Make my poems for others unseen and unborn.
In the day I would be reminded of those men and women
Brave, setting up signals across vast distances,
Considering a nameless way of living, of almost unimagined values.
As the lights darkened, as the lights of night brightened,
We would try to imagine them, try to find each other,
To construct peace, to make love, to reconcile
Waking with sleeping, ourselves with each other.
To reach the limits of ourselves, to reach beyond ourselves,
To let go the means, to wake.

I lived in the first century of these wars.

Muriel Rukeyser, 1913–1980

I first encountered Muriel Rukeyser's 1968 poem in July 2015, when the inimitable Joan Nestle read it to conclude the 'living bibliography' that she presented as part of a panel discussion held at Hares and Hyenas, 'Melbourne's queer and alternative bookshop, cafe and performance space'[1], provocatively entitled 'What is Queer History Good For?'[2]

The event had been lively, thought-provoking, entertaining, uplifting, and spirited. Queer history had been revived, redeemed; its relevance once more revealed and reaffirmed. And yet as the event drew to a close, I became increasingly conscious of an aching, yearning wistfulness that was accompanied by an anxious sense of loss. Part of this was undoubtedly simply the fact that I had enjoyed the discussion, the camaraderie, the sense of *we-feeling* engendered by queerness and its common points of reference temporarily being the norm, rather than the exception. Part of it was the unavoidable return to the outside world and its chilly rain-lashed streets, to be followed by a resumption of the more mundane but no less necessary preoccupations of everyday life. But part of it was a visceral sense that something significant had occurred in hearing Rukeyser's poem, even if I did not yet quite know what it was.

Over the next few weeks, that *something* gradually took form. My knowledge of being had shifted; a previously unarticulated and shapeless thought had found form and, with it, voice: *What would a nameless life be like?* The possibility was as daunting as it was fascinating. Just thinking about it caused a response that was far more felt than thought: a lightening of one's shoulders; a loosening of one's chest and suddenly, almost painfully, being able to breathe deeply for the first time in I-don't-know-when. I felt exhilaration that overwhelmed my mind and swelled my heart, but then bitter grief that choked up my throat and strangled my voice. *This is what could be, but isn't.* The immediate sweet-sourness abated, but tantalising traces remained, an essence to be revisited and savoured anew each time: contemplating the notion of namelessness was freeing, providing momentary relief from the friction of ill-fitting words and potential permission to stop trying to explain oneself to a world that insistently demands we claim names and labels even as it then uses them as simplistic synecdoches to deny the wonderful and troubling complexity and contradiction of our existence and experience. *If you're x, then you're like this. If you're y, then this is who you are. You said you were z. You can't be this and that!*

To experience such a powerful feeling of relief from the idea of not having (or not having to have) a name for one's way of living seems an uncomfortable

---

[1]   https://www.hares-hyenas.com.au/

[2]   http://joannestle2.blogspot.com/2015/07/what-is-queer-history-good-for-public.html

contradiction to the discourses and debates I know from the LGBTIQ+ communities of which I've been part for the past twenty years or so.[3] Acknowledging one's non-heterosexuality and/or gender non-conformity and breaking out of the proverbial closet is supposed to be liberating. We're told that being honest not just with ourselves but with others about our queerness is how we – and others – become able to live authentically and love whole-heartedly. Bravely. *Be yourself! It's hard to be happy when you have to lie about who you are.*[4]

And there is something freeing, even empowering, about explicitly naming the non-normativity of one's desires and the realities of one's existence. *I'm lesbian. I'm gay. I'm bisexual. I'm queer. I'm transgender. I'm genderqueer. I'm asexual.* It's a speech act that has the power to challenge assumptions about gender and of heterosexuality, asserting the fundamental liveability of one's queer life even in the face of flat-out denials. *There's no gay men in Chechnya!*[5] *Bisexuals don't really exist! You're born female; you can't become it!* In voicing ourselves, we loosen norms of straightness and insist that our existence is acknowledged, even if it is not always intelligible to others (Scheman 2011). It is a claiming, a challenge, a cathartic statement: *This is who I am.*

But how to describe that *This*? When? Where? For whom?

So, who am I? To borrow a quip from comedian Hannah Gadsby's recent viral hit *Nanette*[6], more than anything, I'm Tired. I'm tired of the confusion that names cause and the reactions they provoke. I'm tired of having to manage my names in order to bridge the gaps between me and people's expectations and assumptions. I'm tired of being told that *This* cannot be me, because the term woman, female, lesbian, transgender, even queer, is for people who are like *That*. I'm tired of the way that names never quite fit, causing friction on skin, soul, and sensibility. The ways in which they're so often used to divide, police, and blame, to (re)create hierarchies of *(not) real, (not) enough. How gay/queer/trans are you really? Can you prove it?*

Even in supposedly friendly territories, names continue to constrain and contain us under dense and resinous weights of stigma, history, and

---

[3]   More accurately: LGB, then LGBT, then LBT, then LGBTQ, then LGBTQA, then LGBTIQ+.

[4]   https://www.theguardian.com/lifeandstyle/2014/dec/02/the-closet-is-a-terrible-place

[5]   https://www.washingtonpost.com/news/worldviews/wp/2017/07/15/ramzan-kadyrov-says-there-are-no-gay-men-in-chechnya-and-if-there-are-any-they-should-move-to-canada

[6]   https://www.netflix.com/au/title/80233611

multiplying normativities (hetero-, homo-, trans-) as we all anxiously jostle for position and recognition in a body politic that remains ambivalent about our existence, let alone our presence. *I've got nothing against gays, but why do they have to flaunt their sexuality in public? Act normal and you'll be treated normally! There's no such thing as transgender! If you want to know your gender, look in your pants! Genderqueer? Non-binary?! Lefty gender ideology confusing children and perverting the natural order!*

Such weariness of the politics of naming is not, however, to suggest that the absence of names, even if it were possible, would necessarily improve our situation. Rather, it is a call to pause and reflect. As we move further into the second century of global wars, including the ongoing 'Queer Wars' that continue to claim lives and polarise domestically and internationally (Altman and Symons 2016), how do and how don't names work? To turn Juliet's question around, what *isn't* in a name? What are the politics of how we name ourselves as sexual/ised beings and gendered bodies with (or without) desires for intimacy of various kinds? How do names mean and matter? Can we even 'consider a nameless way of living' as something more than a fleeting moment of utopian escapism?

Giving Names

It's a girl! It's a boy! The first name we're assigned is most often not our individual personal name, but a gender. Gender naming marks us, even before birth: once identified as girls, babies risk falling victim to gendercide, adding to the world's estimated 126 million 'missing women' who 'would be alive in the absence of sex discrimination' (Bongaarts and Guilmoto 2015, 242, 246). Those babies whose bodies cannot be easily interpreted as *male* or *female*, meanwhile, risk being surgically 'corrected' to fit restrictive binary categories to be deemed 'normal', with little regard for future identity or pleasure (Amnesty International 2017; Human Rights Watch 2017). Once a gender-name has been assigned, it might not be destiny, but it can certainly shape it, providing an initial stage direction for how we are supposed to perform our innately gendered lives. *Girls like dolls, boys like cars; girls are polite and gentle, boys are forthright and bold; girls are small and delicate, boys are big and strong. Girls become mothers, wives, carers; boys become fathers, husbands, providers.*

This first name hints at future roles embedded in a third name, one left unspoken until it is no longer possible to maintain the assumption of sexual innocence: *heterosexual*. Or, to use its less formal appellation, *straight*. By which we mean sexual desires that are orientated towards persons of the "opposite" sex. This newly uttered name reinforces our gender-names and the supposed complementarity of red-blooded manly men and virtuously womanly women (which is, after all, *only natural*), providing instruction on how to configure intimacy the way society intended. After all, *it's Adam and Eve, not Adam and Steve!*

Of course, the names that society bestows on us at birth by default do not always fit us. We may know it, but the socio-political world around us makes sure we feel it, too. At worst, we are literally named and shamed with spiteful epithets designed to stigmatise and silence: *Fag. Homo. Lesbo. Dyke. Queer. Tranny.* At best, *people like you* are unnamed and all but invisible, their rare appearances in popular culture frequently marked by stereotypes, salaciousness and invasively personal questions. *When did you know you were different? How do you have sex? Have you had the operation?* Even when not marked with malice or well-intentioned but misplaced curiosity, the neo-names utilised cautiously and clinically to try to describe us continue to mark us as *other*, as *not-normal* in how we experience our bodies and our desires. *Homosexual. Transgender. Gender variant. Gender non-conforming. Non-binary. Asexual.* Their aspirational neutrality cannot belie the burden of original names that are uniformly given, nor the damage that they too often cause to bodies, souls, and minds in their reductive normativity.

Claiming Names

Mom, Dad: I need to tell you something... Faced with the chafing of our given names, we may decide to claim a name that better describes our experience of our sexuality and gender. The concept of 'coming out' is at the heart of the modern Western LGBT rights movement. Leaving the closet to live openly as an LGBTIQ person is portrayed as an imperative step towards personal and political liberation and wellbeing (see for example Cheves 2016; Hewlett and Sumberg 2011; Juster et al. 2013; Legate, Ryan and Weinstein 2012). While the imagery of the closet focuses our attention of the physicality and spatiality of the act[7], coming out is as much about being spoken as it is about being seen. Homosexuality is now, to update Lord Alfred Douglas' infamous phrase, the love that dares to speak its name.[8] Indeed, it all but insists upon it: given that appearances, mannerisms or behaviours are not a reliable indication of

---

[7]   See Keith Haring's 1988 National Coming Out Day illustration, for example, in which the figure seems to dance out of the dark into the bright lights, the door flung open http://www.haring.com/!/art-work/national-coming-out-day#.W5DfwoutT-k.

[8]   The original line, "I am the love that dare not speak its name", is the final line of Douglas's 1894 poem, "Two Loves". The phrase is often incorrectly attributed to Oscar Wilde, Douglas's lover, since Wilde was cross-examined about the meaning of the poem while on trial for indecency and sodomy in 1895. While Wilde successfully argued that the poem was about platonic love (he was acquitted), it was (and still is) widely understood as a euphemism for homosexual love.

how someone will describe their sexual orientation and/or gender identity, it is only is it in naming our queerness and disclosing it to others that we fully come into being. *Oh! I've never met a gay person before! No, you have; you just didn't know it...*

The logic of 'I speak, therefore I am' implies that to be nameless is to not exist. Regardless of one's reasons for being there, the closet consigns one to societal invisibility and unknowability, thereby restricting one's ability to live one's truth as a full member of society. As Gabrielle Bellot (2017) argued in response to news in late 2017 that the US Centers for Disease Control had issued advice to avoid certain words like 'transgender' in funding applications, if you 'erase this essential language, you also erase us'. Denial becomes possible, plausible. *We'd heard tales of people like you, but we didn't really believe you existed.* From a socio-political perspective, identities cannot survive without public performance, and re/claiming the names that describe aspects of ourselves which fundamentally shape our everyday interactions in simultaneously profound and banal ways is a vital part of this. Being 'out and proud' about one's sexuality and/or gender identity is thus both a personal and political imperative: to be openly LGBTIQ+ is to exist, to be known, to pledge allegiance to the apparently radical idea that one's embodied reality is valid. *Yes, we exist. No, we won't apologise for existing.*

But names are not only our own. Names are knowledge claims that do not only describe *who* someone is individually, but also *how* they are in the world. Names for one's queerness are the result of tectonic clashes between societal norms and individual selfhood. Formed under great pressure, often violently, the names we use to describe the configurations of our gender identity and sexuality are far more than labels that can be easily attached and removed. Rather, they are transformative, taking the malleable carbon of one's self-knowledge and lived experience and crystallising it into precious diamond-like identities with notionally clean edges, transparent content, and hard, fixed forms: *I'm lesbian. I'm gay. I'm bisexual. I'm queer. I'm transgender. I'm genderqueer. I'm asexual.* These claimed names become hard-won badges of honour and protective talismans that affirm being, confirm identity, combat stigma and restore worth. They are worn with pride: in recognition of personal survival, in solidarity with other queers, in memory of those whose lives were unlived. *We're here, we're queer, get used to it!*

Changing Names

Who are you really? What's your real name? The core implication of such questions is that everyone has a 'true' name that reveals a fundamental essence – not just who someone is, but also how they are. Names are at constant risk of coagulating into definition. How things are here and now is ahistoricised, the past is deleted, the future disavowed. *You as we know you* becomes the standard for how things always were, how they will be and, most dangerously how they *should* be. And names should not be changed! A claimed name may (eventually) be tolerated, but only insofar as it is a correction to reveal the 'real' you, which is fixed and essential. Further attempts at change are met with greater resistance, seen as signs of indecisiveness, inauthenticity or self-indulgent attempts to redefine 'reality' (whatever that may be...).

If given names seek to impose societal command and if claimed names seek to reassert individual autonomy, then changing names requires exposing one's chosen definition of being to public scrutiny – and to the bruising negotiations of the socio-political world. *You can't be gay, you're too manly! You're too pretty to be a lesbian! What do you mean you're neither? Everyone is either male or female! You're too young to know you're transgender! You're confused! It's a just a phase!* In many languages, this disputation over the livability of queer lives often plays out as a proxy war, fought with pronouns lobbed as gender grenades. *What's your husband's name, Katherine?* **Her** *name's Rebecca. ...* **She** *said* **her** *pronouns are* **she, her, hers**! *But* **he** *doesn't look like a* **she**! *... I feel uncomfortable using* **they** *in the singular; it's not proper grammar [translation: it's not proper gender]. ... Look at* **it**, *the f-ing queer!* Even more so that names and pronouns are deployed to police the acceptable borders of gender and sexuality and keep queers in their place. Attempts to carve out space for **they**, **ze, ey, xe** and other gender-neutral pronouns are viewed as disruptive incursions that must be contained so as not to disturb the wider population for whom **he** or **she** is a decision so automatic that it requires no thought – at least, *until those queers turned up with their fancy po-mo ideas about gender and demands for special treatment! Why should* **I** *use pronouns that* **I** *don't believe in? Common courtesy and respect is all very well, but what if everyone wanted* **their** *own pronouns?! It'd be impossible to talk to anyone! It's a queer issue, why should normal people have to deal with* **it***?*

Yet both names and pronouns do change, often in direct defiance of *should, what-ifs* and warnings about slippery slopes. It doesn't happen easily. Great expenditures of time, energy, and emotion are needed to overcome the inertia of existing names and nurture new ones that may be ill-equipped to deal with the harsh climate of the binary-obsessed hetero-homonormative world. Particular exertions are required to dislodge given gender-names and claim one that better fits oneself. Our institutions, invested in upholding the existing gender order, would rather pathologise and punish those who express discontent with their gender assigned at birth rather than seriously consider just how 'normal' a binary conceptualisation of gender really isn't. *I'm all for people expressing themselves, but if a man can claim to be a woman, then what next? It's a slippery slope...* For those who persist and are able to pay the price (and, often, endure the consequent poverty), a new gender-name may eventually be acquired: *transwoman* or *transman*, certainly; maybe even just *man* or *woman* for the more gender-conforming. Sometimes *non-binary* or *genderqueer*, if our systems can cope with it.

Even as our names change, however, they continue to function like maps, flattening and enclosing us. An inevitable reduction has to occur when we put life into words. The changes of name we use to describe our experiences navigating collective grounds become signposts, guiding our interactions and journeys. *Go straight! You are now leaving the hetero-zone. Here be queers. Proceed with caution! Transphobia ahead for the next 10 years and a steep learning gradient with hairpin bends.* The ever-morphing topography of souls and bodies is rendered flat, fixed, readable in the moment. *This, and only this, is who I am/you are here and now.* But these names are meaningful in only abstract, academic, bloodless, emotionless terms. The names we use, these deceptive/ly simple categorisations, obscure the complexity, instability and mess of bodies, loves and lusts. We can keep changing the names we use, time and again, infinitely, but can any name capture a life as it has been lived?

Undoing Names

Perhaps, then, we should not seek to find new names for sexuality and gender identity, but rather get rid of them altogether? Some seem to think so, from the small but growing number of parents raising 'theybies' and trying to keep the dictates of gender-names at bay (Compton 2018; Hanna 2018; Ritschel 2018) to scholars exploring what a post-gender future might look like (Nicholas 2014). It's a case of 'no name, no problem', surely?

Novelist Ursula Le Guin explores this idea in her 1985 short story, *She Unnames Them*. The tale recounts how creatures respond to a proposal 'to give their names back to the people to whom, as they put it, they belonged'. While the majority of wild and domestic animals 'accepted namelessness with the perfect indifference with which they had so long accepted and ignored their names', others such as dogs and parrots maintained 'that their names were important to them, and flatly refused to part with them'. However, as they come to appreciate the politics of unnaming, their perceptions shift:

> But as soon as they understood that the issue was precisely
> one of individual choice, and that anybody who wanted to be
> called Rover, or Froufrou, or Polly, or even Birdie in the

personal sense, was perfectly free to do so, not one of them had the least objection to parting with the lower case (or as regards German creatures, uppercase) generic appellations 'poodle', 'parrot', 'dog', or 'bird', and all the Linnaean qualifiers that had trailed along behind them for two hundred years like tin cans tied to a tail.

Once unnamed, the creatures go about their being much as before. For Le Guin's narrator, however, the effect was a visceral awareness, 'somewhat more powerful than I had anticipated', of what names do:

None were now left to unname, and yet how close I felt to them where I saw one of them swim or fly or trot or crawl across my way or over my skin, or stalk me in the night, or go along beside me for a while in the day. They seemed far closer than when their names had stood between myself and them like a clear barrier: so close that my fear of them and their fear of me became one same fear. And the attraction that many of us felt, the desire to feel or rub or caress one another's scales or skin or feathers or fur, taste one another's blood or flesh, keep one another warm – that attraction was now all one with the fear, and the hunter could not be told from the hunted, nor the eater from the food.

Names, the speaker has realised, create not just order, but structures and hierarchies of power, needs and desires. Names are indicative of place and value, with those better positioned able to assign or outright impose their preferred names – and meanings – on others. *Gay? Pervert! Bisexual? Just greedy! Transgender? Man dressed as a woman! Non-binary? There's no such thing – just look in your pants and you'll know what you really are!*

Despite the loudly-proclaimed progress towards LGBT equality with declarations that 'love is love', to be queer is to know the weight of your name and the cost of your otherness. The pride and power felt in moments of declaration quickly give way to the awareness that there are always unavoidable consequences – sometimes positive, sometimes negative, sometimes fatal – to naming oneself or being named by others. Once voiced, names change reality in ways both tangible and ineffable. Whether voiced proudly, cautiously, casually or fearfully, for the first time or the thousandth (for coming out is an infinite series of moments), naming the orientation of our erotic desires or the (non)-alignment of our gendered bodies with society's tick-box M/F options constitutes an 'altering reality for the self and altering reality for others' (Chirrey 2003, 25). More than anything, attempts at rejecting names heighten our awareness of their power. *Sticks and stones may break my bones, but names can really hurt me.*

Namelessness or Naming-*less*

> What's in a name? that which we call a rose
> By any other name would smell as sweet

> - Shakespeare, W. *Romeo and Juliet,* Act II, Scene II

Shakespeare's Juliet was wrong. Just as our personal names shape perceptions and potentially our choice of profession (Konnikova 2013), the labels that we use to describe our gendered selves and desires smell radically different to different people across time and place. Take *queer,* for example: for many under the LGBTIQA+ umbrella, it has been reclaimed and rehabilitated, its uneasy and fractious polysemy now celebrated for its apparent inclusivity in comparison to the alleged divisiveness of lengthy and lengthening initialisations (Rauch 2019). For others, however, it remains a painful slur that is traumatic rather than liberating, exclusionary rather than inclusive, alienating rather than welcoming (Peron 2016), or a word that is too closely tied to English to have any local resonance or use, other than as a password for access to transnational networks of "global gays" that continue to be dominated by white Europeans and North Americans (Altman 1997). As a name, it is at best a rose with sharp thorns that has just as much capacity to wound as to delight – a fact underscored by the bittersweet recognition that, if there is a common queer experience, then it is that of marginalisation due to one's non-heterosexuality and/or gender non-conformity (Ryan 2016).

Yet while renouncing names may feel like an attractive panacea against the burdens that they impose (and oh how strongly I felt it and wanted the relief of namelessness in that first moment of thought), more sober consideration suggests that such hope is misplaced: upon trying to take her leave from Adam, Le Guin's newly nameless protagonist becomes aware of the consequences of unnaming:

> In fact, I had only just then realised how hard it would have been to explain myself. I could not chatter away as I used to, taking it all for granted. My words must be as slow, as new, as single, as the steps I took going down the path away from the house between the dark-branched, tall dancers motionless against the winter shining.

Names are more powerful borders than any wall could be. These gossamer-light utterances bring imaginary communities into being and divide people into "them" and "us". *Straights/Gays, men/women, cis/trans, queer/normal...* To unname is to undo, to remove the borders that delineate our worlds. Without the reinforcement of names, categories collapse and with them the logic of ownership and property. *The hunter could not be told from the hunted, nor the eater from the food.* Dichotomies of inside/outside, top/bottom, active/passive, powerful/powerless become queered, our unnaming stripping us down to our fundamental desires for touch, for love, for connection, and leaving us vulnerable and exposed. *I'm me and you're you. Isn't that enough?*

Yet renaming, however temporary, is all but unavoidable, if only by dint of practicality and the dependence of communication on common understandings. My final proposal, therefore, is not that we should try to become nameless. Rather, we must cultivate a sensibility and practice of *naming-less* in relation to sexuality and gender that recognises the incompleteness, the transience and the imperfection of names and the political work that names do, hardening around us unbidden and binding our bodies fast with societal norms and borders of all kinds. For, while we cannot escape names and the political baggage with which they travel, lessening the hold of existing names on our lives is a vital step towards creating space for unnamed lives to exist, thereby providing ways out of the current impasse over identity-based rights claims that depend on fixed, binary categories (Altman and Symons 2016, 132–158). With gender and sexuality serving as key battle lines in the second century of these wars, this is one time when less really could be more.

References

Altman, Dennis. 1997. Global Gaze/Global Gays. *GLQ* 3(4): 417–436.

Altman, Dennis and Symons, Jonathan. 2016. *Queer Wars: the new global polarization over gay rights*. Cambridge: Polity Press.

Ambrosino, Brandon. 2017. The invention of 'heterosexuality'. *BBC Future* [online], 16 March, http://www.bbc.com/future/story/20170315-the-invention-of-heterosexuality.

Amnesty International. 2017. *First, Do No Harm: ensuring the Rights of Children with Variations of Sex Characteristics in Denmark*. London: Amnesty International, https://www.amnesty.org/en/documents/eur01/6086/2017/en/.

Bellot, Gabrielle. 2017. The CDC's 7 Word Ban Is an Attempt to Erase Transgender People from Existence. *them.* [online], 18 December, https://www.them.us/story/cdc-ban-erases-transgender-lives.

Bongaarts, John. and Guilmoto, Christophe Z. 2015. How Many More Missing Women? Excess Female Mortality and Prenatal Sex Selection, 1970–2050. *Population and Development Review* 41(2): 241–269.

Cheves, Alexander. 2016. 13 Reasons Why You Must Come Out of the Closet. *The Advocate* [online], 11 October, https://www.advocate.com/coming-out/2016/10/11/13-reasons-why-you-must-come-out-closet.

Chirrey, Deborah A. 2003. 'I hereby come out': What sort of speech act is coming out? *Journal of Sociolinguistics* 7(1): 24–37.

Compton, Julie. 2018. 'Boy or girl?' Parents raising 'theybies' let kids decide. *NBC News* [online], 20 July, https://www.nbcnews.com/feature/nbc-out/boy-or-girl-parents-raising-theybies-let-kids-decide-n891836.

Hanna, Bo. 2018. This Is What It's Like to Raise a Gender-Neutral Child. *Vice* [online], 4 September, https://www.vice.com/en_asia/article/ppxjvb/raising-children-genderneutral-876.

Juster, Robert-Paul; Smith, Nathan G.; Ouellet, Émilie; Sindi, Shireen and Lupien, Sonia J. 2013. Sexual Orientation and Disclosure in Relation to Psychiatric Symptoms, Diurnal Cortisol, and Allostatic Load. *Psychosomatic Medicine* 75(2): 103–116.

Hewlett, Sylvia A. and Sumberg, Karen. 2011. For LGBT Workers, Being 'Out' Brings Advantages. *Harvard Business Review* [online], July-August, https://hbr.org/2011/07/for-lgbt-workers-being-out-brings-advantages.

Human Rights Watch. 2017. *"I Want to Be Like Nature Made Me": Medically Unnecessary Surgeries on Intersex Children in the US*. New York: Human Rights Watch/InterACT, https://www.hrw.org/report/2017/07/25/i-want-be-nature-made-me/medically-unnecessary-surgeries-intersex-children-us.

Konnikova, Maria. 2013. Why Your Name Matters. *The New Yorker*, December 19, https://www.newyorker.com/tech/elements/why-your-name-matters.

Le Guin, Ursula K. 1984. She Unnames Them. *The New Yorker*. January 21: 27, https://www.newyorker.com/magazine/1985/01/21/she-unnames-them.

Legate, Nicole; Ryan, Richard R. and Weinstein, Netta. 2012. Is Coming Out Always a 'Good Thing'? Exploring the Relations of Autonomy Support, Outness, and Wellness for Lesbian, Gay, and Bisexual Individuals. *Social Psychological and Personality Science* 3(2): 145–152.

Nicholas, Lucy. 2014. *Queer Post-Gender Ethics: The Shape of Selves to Come*. Basingstoke: Palgrave Macmillan.

Peron, James. 2016. Not Queer, Just Gay. No, Thanks. *Huffington Post* [online], February 3, https://www.huffingtonpost.com/james-peron/not-queer-just-gay-no-thanks_b_9145566.html.

Rauch, Jonathan. 2019. It's Time to Drop the 'LGBT' From 'LGBTQ'. *The Atlantic* [online], January/February, https://www.theatlantic.com/magazine/archive/2019/01/dont-call-me-lgbtq/576388/.

Ritschel, Chelsea. 2018. Couple Raises Child as a Gender-Neutral 'They-by'. *Independent* [online], 3 April, https://www.independent.co.uk/life-style/health-and-families/theyby-gender-neutral-child-parents-raise-couple-kyl-myers-zoomer-a8286876.html.

Ryan, Hugh. 2016. Why Everyone Can't Be Queer. *Slate* [online], 14 July. http://www.slate.com/blogs/outward/2016/07/14/why_jenna_wortham_s_queer_article_misunderstands_the_marginalization_in.html.

Scheman, Naomi. 2011. Queering the Centre by Centring the Queer: Reflections in Transsexuals and Secular Jews. In: Scheman, Naomi. *Shifting Ground: Knowledge and Reality, Transgression and Trustworthiness*. Oxford: Oxford University Press: 111–144.

2

Japanese 'LGBT Boom' Discourse and its Discontents

IOANA FOTACHE

Introduction[1]

In the summer of 2016, I went inside a small café to talk to the owners about a local LGBT[2] campaign: 'Excuse me, do you know what LGBT means?' They didn't. I tried again, asking about *sekushuaru mainoriti*[3], then *seiteki mainoriti*[4], then the fully native term, *seiteki shōsūsha*[5]. The owner somewhat understood the latter, but asked me to be more specific. I explained that I was referring to people who love people of the same-sex or whose gender identity does not match their biological identity. The owner then exclaimed: 'Oh! Is this about *homos*[6]?' From a cross-cultural perspective, Japan is often portrayed

---

[1]   When transcribing Japanese, macrons (⌒) are used to show when a vowel should be prolonged in pronunciation. Japanese names are written in Japanese order, with the surname first. The Japanese language uses three types of character sets: Kanji (Chinese characters) and two syllabaries; loanwords are usually transcribed phonetically, rather than translated, and some loanwords are abbreviated or acquire alternate meanings, a process referred to as *wasei eigo* (Japanised English). Given the phonetic nature of these words, speakers unfamiliar to the word would not understand its meaning intuitively.

[2]   I use the term 'queer' to refer collectively to all sexual and gender minorities. Additionally, though the queer community can be referred to as LGBTQ, LGBTQIA+, etc., the term *LGBT* will be used throughout this chapter, given its current use as the default term in Japanese discourse. The term 'sexual minority' has come under criticism for grouping sexual and gender minorities under the same umbrella, but its uses and political intricacies are beyond the scope of this article.

[3]   Phonetic rendition of *sexual minority*.

[4]   Native term for *sexual (and gender)*, phonetic rendition of *minority*.

[5]   Fully native term for *sexual minority*.

[6]   The Japanese term *homo* and the English term *homo* have the same etymological

as a comparatively tolerant country due to the scarcity of LGBT-related hate crime and active persecution (Vincent, Kazama and Kawaguchi 1997, 170). However, discrimination exists at a systemic and institutional level, as Japan does not have an anti-discrimination law, same-sex partnerships are only recognised to a limited extent in certain cities, and workplace discrimination, bullying, and suicide rates continue to be a problem for the queer population. The current consensus seems to be that queer culture is tolerated, so long as it stays segregated and does not disturb the majority (Equaldex n.d.; Hidaka et al. 2008; Taniguchi 2006; Vincent, Kazama and Kawaguchi 1997).

In addition to their fight for human rights within a national context, the queer community is facing an additional internal struggle regarding their direction, approach, and even terminology. 'Global queering' and the formation of the 'global gay' have become a topic of interest surrounding the formation of queer identities and sexualities in Asia as globalisation has paved the way for new cultural flows between queer communities around the globe (Altman 1996; Jackson 2009). Though Western influence over the understanding of Japanese sexuality and relationships has been present since the late nineteenth century, the 'global gay' and its identity politics is said to have become particularly noticeable in Japan since the 1990s. Until then, the Japanese queer community had evolved differently than the Western model, intertwined but facing different obstacles, developing separate terminologies and performances (McLelland 2000, 2005). A paradigm shift occurred in 2010, which saw an almost full switch from local terminology and discourse to Anglicised terms and symbolism that gained national attention, in what is informally referred to as the *LGBT Boom* (Horie 2015).

This chapter offers a short overview of queer discourse in Japan, the state and terminology of the LGBT Boom, and its position within national and global queer discourse.

Queer History in Japan

Though cases of same-sex love, cross-dressing, and individuals living as genders different from what was assigned at birth are documented throughout premodern Japanese history, they do not match current understandings of gay or transgender identities, as they were consolidated within strict social roles, linked to lifestyle or religious occupations, not placed within a heterosexual dichotomy, and referred almost exclusively to males (Horie 2015, 199–200; Itani 2011, 284–285; McLelland 2011).

---

formation, history, and negative connotation. The Japanese queer community considers it a slur.

In the late nineteenth century, Japan adopted many Western values in the handling of relationships, institutions, familial relations, and social values, which extended to public stances on homosexuality. Though the Japanese sodomy law was lifted after only twelve years, the taboo lived on in the public consciousness, and transsexualism was pathologised (McLelland 2000, 22–25; Itani 2011, 285–286; Mitsuhashi 2003, 103). Removed from the public sphere, Japanese queer culture steadily developed throughout the twentieth century in bars, underground magazines, and an entertainment sector mostly consisting of gay men and crossdressers (Yonezawa 2003; McLelland 2005).

Attempts to politicise their discourse and form alternate communities are noticeable starting in the 1970s, within grassroots gatherings, gay magazines, and the occasional breach into politics or mainstream entertainment (McLelland et al. 2007; Sawabe 2008; Sugiura 2006). However, it wasn't until the 1990s that a wider political LGBT discourse formed.

In what is informally known as the 'Gay Boom', the 1990s saw a considerable increase in media portrayals of queer characters, as well as manifestos and autobiographies from members of the LGBT community. Simultaneously, local and international organisations were involved in combating HIV/AIDS, and advocacy groups took the first steps to legally combat LGBT discrimination and advocate for a national queer discourse, leading to the idea of identitarian sexuality taking form in Japan.

Most notably, transgender advocates achieved a series of successes starting in the mid-1990s: Gender Identity Disorder (GID) was translated into Japanese in 1996, which led to the legalisation of sex reassignment surgery (Itani 2011, 282). In 2003, trans woman Kamiwaka Aya became the first elected Japanese LGBT politician, and worked to introduce a law which allowed trans citizens to change their gender in the Official Family Register. While severely limited, this set a precedent as the first legal recognition of queer people in Japan, (Kamikawa 2007; Taniguchi 2013). Where the term 'sexual minorities' previously represented gay or crossdressing men, the medical and political backing of the transgender rights movement had managed to turn the concept of sexual minorities into a placeholder for people suffering from GID in the public eye (Horie 2015, 196). At the same time, lesbian, gay, intersex, asexual, and other queer groups continued solidifying throughout the 2000s, both locally and online (Dale 2012; Fushimi 2003, 197–224; Hirono 1998; 'The History of Asexuality in Japan' n.d.). The politics of coming out gradually entered the movement's consciousness, though it has yet to be readily embraced by the general population.

The term 'LGBT' rapidly spread in vernacular activism in the 2010s (Horie

2015, 167), and the election of two more gay public officials in 2011 seemed to solidify the LGBT movement's political direction. Pride celebrations spread across the country, and over 70,000 people attended the Tokyo parade[7]. The international wave of civil partnership laws prompted discussion among the national policy-makers, and Shibuya ward in Tokyo was the first to make them official in 2015[8], followed by another five districts and cities the following year. The 2016–2017 election season brought another four LGBT politicians into city councils and even the national assembly. By 2018, it seemed that Japan had managed to establish a solid queer presence that breached into mainstream politics.

Despite the LGBT Boom's unprecedented success, queer people themselves are not always in line with its discourse. Within the community, a counter-discourse is forming around members who are against LGBT Boom goals and values such as same-sex marriage, coming out, focus on visibility and assimilation, and the terminology of the discourse itself. The following section is concerned with the terminology and symbolism that are currently employed by the Japanese queer community, and how they entered the vernacular.

Queer Terminology and Symbolism in Japan

Loanwords in the queer community are not a recent phenomenon. The first mention of homosexuality in modern Japanese society relied on the term *uruningu[9]*, brought in by Mori Ōgai from Germany (McLelland 2000, 22), and foreign terms such as *pederasuto/pede[10]*, *lezubosu[11]*, *safisuto[12]*, *daiku[13]*, and *burū bōi[14]* were used sporadically throughout the decades (McLelland et al. 2007). However, these terms were used exclusively within queer spaces, especially in gay bars and cruising sites. Most of the currently used LGBT terms were initially adopted in the post-war period, but their meanings and extent have shifted considerably; it was during the Gay Boom that queer terminology took a more definitive Anglocentric approach, and previous

---

[7] Following (or perhaps starting) the shift in vernacular, the *Tokyo Gay and Lesbian Parade* changed its name to *Tokyo Rainbow Pride.*

[8] It should be noted that the legal recognition of these civil partnerships is virtually non-existent, though they are often referred to as 'same-sex partnerships': they are not recognised nationally, and only offer a limited amount of recognition and rights to the individuals who register for it.

[9] Phonetic rendition of *urning,* a German term used to describe same-sex lovers in early sexology.

[10] Phonetic rendition of *pederast.*

[11] Phonetic rendition of *lesbos.*

[12] Phonetic rendition of *Sappho.*

[13] Phonetic rendition of *dyke.*

[14] *Blue boy,* a term that became popular in the 1950s and 1960s after a Paris play.

terminology (borrowed and native alike) started to be considered archaic, old-fashioned, or derogatory. The change was amplified by the efforts of queer activist groups in changing and adopting Japanese queer terminology in a direction that separates it from allusions to femininity, prostitution, and medicalised jargon (Lunsing 2005, 82–83). To keep up with the shifting terminology, members of the community employ various tactics.

One way in which activists confront the linguistic barrier is through the constant explanation of terms. Many queer websites and pamphlets feature explanations of the terms in a visible area; the following is a typical example, as seen in a pamphlet advertising IDAHO (the International Day Against Homophobia, Transphobia and Biphobia):

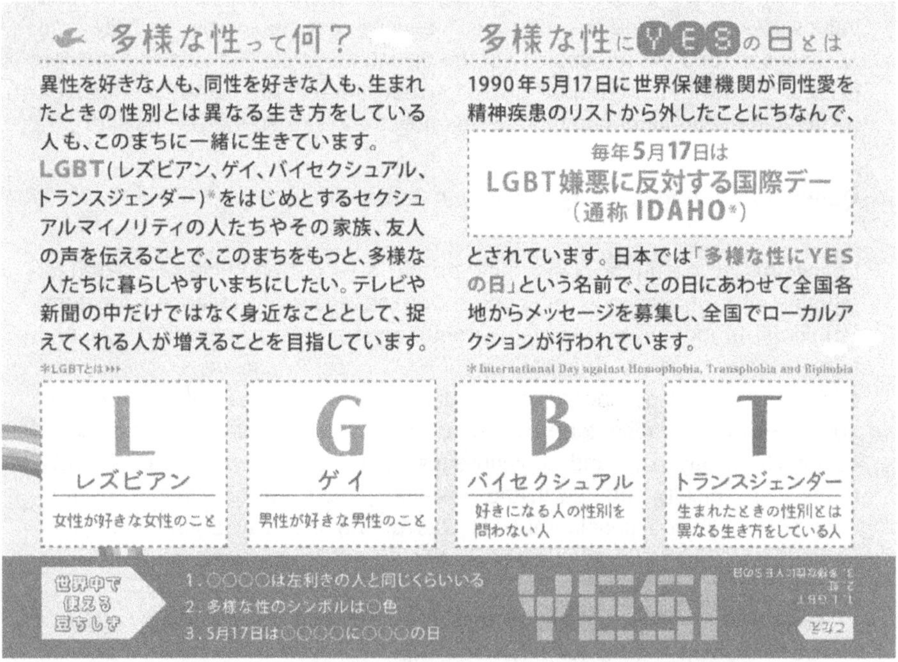

Figure 1. The back of a pamphlet advertising IDAHO, called 'say YES to sexual diversity day' in Japan. From '5 gatsu 17 nichi ha「tayou na sei ni YES no hi」！' by Yappa AiDAHO[15], 2018. Copyright 2018 by Yappa AiDAHO idaho.net. Reproduced with permission.

Explanations start by singling out the letters of the LGBT acronym in the Roman alphabet, then rendering it phonetically, followed by a short

15 https://idaho0517.jimdo.com/

explanation of the meaning either mechanically (women who love women, men who love men, people whose lifestyle does not match the one assigned at birth, etc.) or using native terms. Often, they add an explanation as to why the native or commonly used terms are considered inappropriate.

Activists are currently in favour of LGBT terminology, despite the linguistic barrier. This is mainly due to the history of these terms and their development within – and especially outside – the community. The following is a breakdown of how L,G,B, and T entered the Japanese vernacular, and what they are meant to replace.

L

> I knew the words '*homo*' and '*rezu*'[16], but they were just perverted words that I learned in primary school. (Ōtsuji 2005, 54)

As the Japanese language does not feature the letter *L*, *lesbian* has entered the language as *rezubian*. However, advocates have chosen to keep the letter L in the term *LGBT*.

The word *rezubian* was first recorded in Japan in 1963, referring to a female bartender dressed as a man (Sugiura 2006, 130). Later, its abbreviation, *rezu*, became associated with male-oriented pornography, though it was one of the many terms employed by grassroots lesbian movements starting in the 1970s. *Rezubian* as a self-named identity took over during the 1990s (Horie 2015). One major problem that it faced was the negative connotation that the word *rezubian* (especially *rezu*) had for being used by male-targeted lesbian pornography – not only did lesbians have to inform others of their existence, but they had to erase the previous negative usage of the word (Kakefuda 1992). *Rezubian* was shortened to *bian* by the Lesbian community around the mid-1990s, as they wanted to refer to themselves using a word that discarded its mainstream connotation. Unlike *rezu*, which continues to be used in pornography or as a derogatory term, *bian* has not successfully entered the mainstream language, and is mostly used as a lavender term within the community.

G

> 'Tsuyoshi, are you *homo*?'

---

[16] *Rezu* is the Japanese equivalent of 'lezzie': an abbreviation of *rezubian*/lesbian that is casually used in a derogatory manner.

'Yeah, but since *homo* isn't a good word, call me *gei*[17]'. (Ryoji and Sunagawa 2007, 51–52)

Homo entered the Japanese language in the 1920s, and has maintained a fairly constant derogatory connotation since, though its presence continues to be strong in popular media. The word *gei* first entered the language in the postwar period and was used to refer to *gei boi*[18], male sex workers and crossdressers working in designated bars. It wasn't until the Gay Boom that *gei* became associated with male-identified homosexuals, but it has since become the preferred term to refer to men who love men.

The native term *dōseiaisha*[19] is still used to refer to male homosexuals, although some find it too medical-sounding or criticise its tendency to refer to gay men and women alike (Ishikawa 2011).

B

As is unfortunately the case with queer communities around the world, bisexual erasure is quite common in the Japanese queer community, as bisexuals are caught in the divide between heterosexuals and homosexuals and become either assimilated or shunned (Matsunaga 1998). Given the divide between married life and sexual enjoyment, people who have affairs with the same-sex, but marry a member of the opposite sex do not take on the bisexual identity, but either identify as homosexual or 'grow out of it' (McLelland 2000). Though bisexuality is always included when explaining the term LGBT, for the most part they are absent from general discussions and movements. The native term *ryōseiaisha*[20] (or *zenseiaisha*[21] for pansexuals) exists, but it is simply not used as much as *baisekushuaru*[22] or *bai* [23](Hirono 1998).

T

'Oi, Okama[24]!'

---

[17]   Phonetic rendition of *gay*.
[18]   Phonetic rendition of *gay boy*.
[19]   Lit. 'same-sex lover'.
[20]   Lit. 'lover of both sexes'.
[21]   Lit. 'lover of all sexes'.
[22]   Phonetic rendition of *bisexual*.
[23]   Phonetic rendition of *bi*.
[24]   Lit. an archaic term for buttocks that has been in use since the Edo period to describe men who have sex with men and crossdressers.

[...] 'Uhm, "Okama" is slightly different. "Okama" was originally a feminine man, so I guess I would be an "onabe", right? Oh, but "onabe" is pretty tied to the entertainment industry, much like "new half", so once again it's not really me. By the way, if you call me a lesbian then that's not really right, either (Sugiyama 2007, 207).

Before the 1990s, transgender (and crossdressing) individuals were referred to using the terms *okama*, *gei boi*, *onee*[25], or *nyū hāfu*[26]. The lesbian community used the word *onabe*[27] to refer to butch lesbians initially, though that term evolved to describe FtMs (female to male) around the mid-1990s (Sugiura 2006).

The word *toransujendā*[28] is said to have been introduced in 1994, with the narrow sense of a full-time biologically male crossdresser who did not wish to undergo sex reassignment surgery (Itani 2011, 288). Transgender individuals who decided to transition referred to themselves as *toransekushuaru*[29]. Transgender individuals who did not transition at all, or lived a double life, were derogatorily referred to as *toransuvesutaito*[30], often abbreviated as TV.

Toransujendā became the preferred term within the community in the 2000s, alongside the English acronyms of FtM and MtF[31]. This change mirrored the Western debate, which underwent a similar transformation of preferred terms. The Japanese trans community did not, however, extend *Toransujendā* to cover the entire trans umbrella to include non-binary identities.

Despite the derogatory connotations, there are some transgender individuals who willingly refer to themselves as *okama, onabe,* or *nyū hāfu*, and they are still the most commonly used words in Japanese society. However, advocates posit that these terms are more often used as slurs or are restricted to the entertainment industry. *Okama*, in particular, being a well-known term, is used as a slur against gay men, intersex individuals, and other queer groups alike (Fushimi 2003).

---

[25] Big sister.

[26] From *New Half,* a term that was popularised in the 1970s by crossdressing entertainers as someone who is half of both genders.

[27] This is a play upon words. *Kama* has switched meanings from 'buttocks' to a type of pot in modern Japan. *Nabe* is yet another type of Japanese pot. Therefore, *onabe* refers to them being a different kind of *okama*.

[28] Phonetic rendition of *transgender*.

[29] Phonetic rendition of *transsexual*.

[30] Phonetic rendition of *transvestite*.

[31] Interestingly, non-binary individuals (who identify as *X-gender*) use the same naming system, calling themselves MtX or FtX.

The most problematic aspect regarding native terms for trans individuals is that there is no word used to describe a transgender person. Even though GID was replaced with gender dysphoria in the DSM-V, the term *GID* is widely used, often as a placeholder for gender-non-conforming individuals. When explaining the *T* in *LGBT*, advocates use descriptions such as 'a person suffering from GID', 'a person whose sex does not match their gender', etc., but it is not uncommon to refer to the individual simply as 'GID', even within the community. Due to the focus on GID as a pillar for the transgender movement's legitimacy, *TG/TV* people are still often separated from *TS* depending on their desire to undergo sex reassignment surgery (or not): non-cisgender individuals who do not desire medical treatment are not seen as 'real' representatives of their community.

Symbols

The Anglocentric influence is not limited to word usage: it also affects symbols. In 2017, all the queer parades in the country relied on international symbolism and terms: the Tokyo Rainbow Parade, the Nagoya Rainbow Parade, the Kyushu Rainbow Pride, the Sapporo Rainbow March, the Kumamoto Pride, the Kansai Rainbow Festa, the Aomori Pride, the Okinawa Pink Dot[32], and many non-profit organisations use the words *Pride*, *Diversity*, or *Rainbow* in their names.

There is a great discrepancy between the use of the rainbow as a queer symbol and the rainbow in mainstream media. Despite the heavy use of rainbows within the queer community, the rainbow is not seen as a queer symbol in mainstream discourse: colourful rainbows are often employed as decorations in Japan. For example, while Nagoya Rainbow Week 2016 used the rainbow to paint itself as a queer event, the Aichi Trienalle 2016 edition called 'Rainbow Caravan'[33] took place simultaneously in the same city centre, with no queer context behind it. It was thus easy for passersby to consider the Nagoya Rainbow Week an art event that was related to the Trienalle, rather than a stand-alone queer event.

Similarly, words such as *puraido*[34] or *daibāshitī*[35] can be a barrier: one needs to first understand the word *pride/diversity* in English, then to know its political connotation within the international queer community. It is difficult to figure out exactly when Pride and rainbows made their way into Japan due to the

---

[32]   Named after the Pink Dot festival in Singapore.

[33]   One of the largest art festivals in Japan, held every three years in the city of Nagoya, Aichi prefecture.

[34]   Phonetic rendition of *pride*.

[35]   Phonetic rendition of *diversity*.

scarce literature on the matter, but their popularity has escalated since the 2010s (Welker 2010).

Anglicisation or Hybridity?

In the 1990s, the international HIV/AIDS movement helped establish a precedent in countries where homosexuality had been previously ignored or even prosecuted. But in doing so it has become a tool susceptible to globalisation and the promotion of an international gay/lesbian agenda based on a Western/US model (Altman 1996). This trend was accused of dividing international gay formations from local homosexualities, causing an identity crisis among the native population who felt pressured to replace their local identities with Western LGBT ones. Critics of global queering encouraged caution and the need to include non-Eurocentric perspectives into the definition of sexuality. A counter-discourse to global queering as a hegemonic force pointed out that it assumes a strict dichotomy between East/West, dominator/dominated, etc., and that it overstates the influence of the West over Asian discourse. As maintained by this view, rather than imposed, Western categories are assimilated and redefined according to local values in a process of queer hybridity (Boellstorff and Leap 2004; Martin et al. 2008).

Westerners tend to perceive English terms in Asian cultures as proof of Westernisation, but in doing so they disregard the changes that these terms have undergone locally. Though globalisation is often associated with homogenisation/Anglicisation, developments in local contexts contribute to a multidimensional understanding of values on a transnational, rather than universal, scale. Understanding contemporary queer movements in Asia as mere imitations greatly oversimplifies the matter. While it is true that English terms have become part of the local queer discourse, they do not always fully mirror their Western equivalents, and as we can see, they were not adopted overnight, but rather as a result of ongoing negotiations and discourse development (Jackson 2009; Wilson 2006).

Shimizu Akiko (2007) states that we cannot really talk about global queering in the case of Japan, since there were no instances of native understandings of queer identities outside a Western frame to begin with. The borrowing and redefinition of English terminology according to local standards can be seen in Japan over the decades, where locals used their own subjective experience to define and redefine their sexual identity and its name. This exchange has been fueled first by international exchanges and transnational organisations, but the result was always a hybrid between the Western model and local subjectivities. However, it is important to note that this debate was mostly carried out before the 2010 LGBT Boom, which emulates Western terminology and tactics to a wider extent.

While its strategic use has proved successful in national politics, media, and recognition, it is important to evaluate how well it resonates with Japan's queer population. Otherwise, the LGBT Boom risks alienating the members it claims to represent, while also failing to reach out to a wider Japanese audience, since it relies on terms and premises that the locals do not necessarily recognise. Additionally, the focus on same-sex partnership and coming out has also been adopted to imitate the Western ideals of the queer agenda, but the question must be raised deeper within the Japanese context.

Hybrid or not, the Anglocentric terminology is not just an issue of linguistic historicity, but has become a linguistic barrier within the community. According to a survey performed by the Japan LGBT Research Institute (2016), only 49.8% of the respondents who identified as non-cisgender and non-hetero knew what the LGBT acronym meant, and those unfamiliar with Western LGBT culture and terminology are unlikely to recognise the terms or symbols when they see them. Current queer terminology in Japan has become diglossic, as native terms are considered pathological, derogatory, or old-fashioned (even though they see use within the community), whereas the English terms are seen as empowering due to their international symbolism.

Conclusion

I raise these issues not to entirely dismiss the LGBT Boom discourse, but to present a more comprehensive picture of the current state of the community and its discourse. As Shimizu (2005) points out, reactionary radical resistance to the Anglocentric terms is not necessarily promoting local movements, so much as stagnating political advancement in favour of polemics outside the scope of the actual movement. It is true that the uncritical adoption of international terminology carries the risk of normativisation, rendering subjectivities invisible. However, one must be careful when dismissing the model employed by Japanese activists as strictly Western: it can be seen as merely a strategic tool employed by activists to stir up debate, rather than to overwrite native identities (Suganuma 2007, 495–496).

The separation between political queer discourse and local behaviour has long existed (Horie 2015, 65; Shimizu 2007, 508–510), so perhaps this Western discourse/local acts divide is just continuing that trend, trying to gain the strategic advantage in mainstream discourse whilst allowing native queer culture to develop. It was there during the Gay Boom, it is here during the LGBT Boom. What is necessary is more awareness regarding the gap between identity politics discourse and those it represents.

The current confusion doesn't have to be permanent, and attempts to combine approaches are already underway. Since the 1990s, a steady stream of autobiographies have been released, in which activists and public figures merge identity politics with their subjective experience, all while explaining queer terminology and how they feel about it (Fushimi 1991; Kakefuda 1992; Kamikawa 2007; Ōtsuji 2005; Sugiyama 2011). Though it is still a work in progress, activists are working on reaching out to a wider audience using introductory books, mangas, and videos on queer issues (Harima et al. 2013; Hidaka 2014; Ishida et al. 2010; Ishikawa 2011). Moreover, institutional efforts seek to raise LGBT awareness in schools and workplaces, offering access to information and allowing new venues for discussion. Hopefully, the confusion and polemics are merely a phase that will be remembered as a footnote in Japanese queer history, rather than a definite divide.

References

Altman, Dennis. 1996. "On Global Queering." *Australian Humanities Review* 2: 1–9.

Boellstorff, Tom, and William L. Leap. 2004. *Speaking in Queer Tongues: Globalization and Gay Language*. Champaign, IL: University of Illinois Press.

Dale, S.P.F. 2012. "An Introduction to *X-Jendā*: Examining a New Identity in Japan." *Intersections: Gender and Sexuality in Asia and the Pacific* 31: n.p. http://intersections.anu.edu.au/issue31/dale.htm#t19.

Equaldex. n.d. "LGBT Rights in Japan." *Equaldex*. Accessed November 27, 2016. http://www.equaldex.com/region/japan.

Fushimi, Noriaki. 1991. *Puraibēto Gei Raifu*. Tokyo, Japan: Gakuyō Shobō.

Fushimi, Noriaki. 2003. *Hentai (kuia) Nyuumon*. Tokyo, Japan: Chikuma.

Harima, Katsuki, Toshiyuki Ōshima, Aki Nomiya, Masae Torai, and Aya Kamikawa. 2013. *Sei Dōitsusei Shōgai to Koseki : Seibetsu Henkō to Tokureihō O Kangaeru*. Tokyo, Japan: Ryokufū Shuppan.

Hidaka, Yasuharu. 2014. *Anata Ga Anatarashiku Ikiru Tame Ni - Seiteki Mainoriti to Jinken*. Tokyo, Japan: Tōei. https://www.youtube.com/watch?v=G9DhghaAxlo.

Hidaka, Yasuharu, Don Operario, Mie Takenaka, Sachiko Omori, Seiichi

Ichikawa, and Takuma Shirasaka. 2008. "Attempted Suicide and Associated Risk Factors among Youth in Urban Japan." *Social Psychiatry and Psychiatric Epidemiology* 43 (9): 752–57.

Hirono, Maki. 1998. "Baisekushuaru Ni Tsuite No Q&A [Bisexual Q&A]." In *Anata, Okama, Kirai?*. Osaka, Japan: Project P. http://barairo.net/works/TEXT/bifaq.html#Anchor-Q8.

Ishida, Ira, Sonin, Fumino Sugiyama, Kenichirou Mogi, Frankie Lily, Pico, Sachiko Takeuchi, Katsuki Harima, and Toshiaki Hirata. 2010. *NHK「hāto Wo tsunagou」LGBT BOOK*. Tokyo, Japan: Ōta shuppan.

Ishikawa, Taiga. 2011. *Gei No Boku Kara Tsutaetai Suki No Wakaru Hon - Minna Gashinranai LGBT*. Tokyo, Japan: Tarō Jirōsha Editasu.

Itani, Satoko. 2011. "Sick but Legitimate? Gender Identity Disorder and a New Gender Identity Category in Japan." In *Sociology of Diagnosis*, edited by PJ McGann and David J. Hutson, 281 – 306. Bingley, UK: Emerald Group.

Jackson, Peter A. 2009. "Global Queering and Global Queer Theory: Thai [trans] Genders and [homo] Sexualities in World History."*Autrepart* 1: 15–30.

Japan LGBT Research Institute. 2016. "Hakuhōdō DY gurūpu no kabushikigaisha LGBT sōgōkenkyūsho, 6 tsuki 1-nichi kara no sābisu kaishi ni atari LGBT o hajime to suru sekusharumainoriti no ishiki chōsa o jisshi". Tokyo, Japan: Kawadeshobōshinsha.

Kamikawa, Aya. 2007. *Kaete Yuku Yūki : "Sei Dōitsusei Shōgai" No Watakushi Kara* . Tokyo, Japan: Iwanami.

Lunsing, Wim. 2005. "The Politics of Okama and Onabe: Uses and Abuses of Terminology Regarding Homosexuality and Transgender." In *Genders, Transgenders, and Sexualities in Japan*, 81–95. New York, NY: Routledge.

Martin, Fran, Peter A. Jackson, Mark McLelland, and Audrey Yue, eds. 2008. *AsiaPacifiQueer: Rethinking Genders and Sexualities*. Chicago, IL: University of Illinois Press.

Matsunaga, Kazumi. 1998. "A Bisexual Life." In *Queer Japan: Personal Stories of Japanese Lesbians, Gays, Transsexuals, and Bisexuals*, edited by Barbara Summerhawk, Cheiron McMahill, and Darren McDonald, 37–45. New Victoria

Publishers.

McLelland, Mark J. 2011. "Japan's Queer Cultures." In *The Routledge Handbook of Japanese Culture and Society*, edited by Victoria Bestor and Theodore Bestor, 140–49. New York, NY: Routledge.

McLelland, Mark J. 2000. *Male Homosexuality in Modern Japan: Cultural Myths and Social Realities*. Richmond, UK: Curzon Press.

McLelland, Mark J. 2005. *Queer Japan from the Pacific War to the Internet Age*. Lanham, MD: Rowman & Littlefield.

Mitsuhashi, Junko. 2003. "Nihon Toransujenda Ryakushi (sono 1) - Kodai Kara Kindai Made." In *Toransujendarizumu Sengen: Seibetsu No Jikotteiken to Tayō Na Sei No Koutei*, edited by Yonezawa, 104–18. Tokyo, Japan: Shakaihihyōsha.

McLelland, Mark, Katsuhiko Suganuma, and James Welker. 2007. *Queer Voices from Japan: First Person Narratives from Japan's Sexual Minorities*. Lanham, MD: Lexington Books.

Ryoji, Sunagawa and Hideki Sunagawa. 2007. *Coming out Letters*. Tokyo, Japan: Tarō Jirōsha.

Sawabe, Hitomi. 2008. "The Symbolic Tree of Lesbianism in Japan: An Overview of Lesbian Activist History and Literary Works." In *Sparkling Rain: And Other Fiction from Japan of Women Who Love Women*, edited by Barbara Summerhawk and Kimberly Hughes, translated by Kimberly Hughes, 2–16. Chicago, IL: New Victoria Publishers.

Shimizu, Akiko. 2005. "The Catch in Indigenousness, Or What Is Wrong with 'Asian Queers'." *Inter-Asia Cultural Studies* 6 (2): 301–3.

Shimizu, Akiko. 2007. "Scandalous Equivocation: A Note on the Politics of Queer Self-naming." *Inter-Asia Cultural Studies* 8 (4): 503–16.

Suganuma, Katsuhiko. 2007. "Associative Identity Politics: Unmasking the Multi-Layered Formation of Queer Male Selves in 1990s Japan." *Inter-Asia Cultural Studies* 8 (4): 485–502.

Sugiura, Ikuko. 2006. "Lesbian Discourses in Mainstream Magazines of Post-War Japan: Is Onabe Distinct from Rezubian?" *Journal of Lesbian Studies* 10 (3-4): 127–44.

Sugiyama, Fumino. 2009. *Double Happiness.* Tokyo, Japan: Kōdansha.

Ōtsuji, Kanako. 2005. *Kamingu Auto : Jibunrashisa O Mitsukeru Tabi.* Tokyo, Japan: Kōdansha.

Horie, Yuri. 2015. *Lesbian Identities.* Tokyo, Japan: Rakuhoku.

"Nihon No Asekushuaru No Kako [The History of Asexuality in Japan]." n.d. Asexual.jp. Accessed November 25, 2016. http://www.asexual.jp/history_japan.php.

Taniguchi, Hiroyuki. 2006. "The Legal Situation Facing Sexual Minorities in Japan." *Intersections: Gender, History and Culture in the Asian Context* 12: n.p. http://intersections.anu.edu.au/issue12/taniguchi.html#t1.

Taniguchi, Hiroyuki. 2013. "Japan's 2003 Gender Identity Disorder Act: The Sex Reassignment Surgery, No Marriage, and No Child Requirements as Perpetuations of Gender Norms in Japan." *Asian - Pacific Law & Policy Journal* 14 (2): 108–117.

Vincent, Keith, Kazuya Kawaguchi, and Takashi Kazama. 1997. *Gay Studies.* Tokyo, Japan: Seidōsha.

Welker, James. 2010. "Telling Her Story: Narrating a Japanese Lesbian Community." *Journal of Lesbian Studies* 14 (4): 359–80.

Wilson, Ara. 2006. "Intersections: Queering Asian." *Intersections: Gender, History and Culture in the Asian Context* 14 (November): n.p. http://intersections.anu.edu.au/issue14/wilson.html#t32.

Yappa AiDAHO idaho.net. 2018. "Download Pamphlet." 5 Gatsu 17 Nichi Haﾞtayou Na Sei Ni YES No Hiﾞ. 2018. https://idaho0517.jimdo.com

Yonezawa, Izumi. 2003. *Toransujendarizumu.* Tokyo, Japan: Shakaihihyōsha.

3

Translating 'Queer' Into (Kyrgyzstani) Russian

MOHIRA SUYARKULOVA

Introduction

As Gayatri Spivak famously wrote, 'In every possible sense, translation is necessary but impossible' (2007, 263). This chapter contributes to this idea by looking at how a foreign term like 'queer' has been translated, appropriated, and utilised in Kyrgyzstani discourses and practices of gender and sexual 'dissidents'. In particular, I examine the translatability of the term 'queer' and the challenges associated with such an attempt to translate. I contend that far from being derivative, *kvir* in Kyrgyzstan (and beyond – in the post-Soviet space) is utilised in unique ways as part of ideological interventions and debates in activist circles. I explore the intersection between translation, political activism, and global queer politics by looking at the case of the word *kvir* in Kyrgyzstan.

The analysis here stems from my personal experience using Russian-English and English-Russian translations as a form of political activism while living and working in Kyrgyzstan between 2012 and 2017. The Russian language remains a *lingua franca* of the post-Soviet space and has the status of official language in the Kyrgyz Republic, along with the Kyrgyz language, which has the status of 'state language' (having a higher ideological status). I have translated iconic publications of feminist and queer history from English to Kyrgyz – such as Adrienne Rich's famous essay "Compulsory heterosexuality and lesbian existence" (1980/2014) and *Queer Nation Manifesto* (1990/2016). I have also translated the Kyrgyzstan-based School of Theory and Activism Bishkek's (STAB) "Queer Communism Manifesto" (2013). Why do I use translation as activism? And what role does translation play in the global politics of gender and sexuality? How can one translate 'queer' into Kyrgyzstani Russian?

It is common in both Russian and English literary translation tradition to praise works that are marked by fluency, creating an illusion that one is indeed reading an original text rather than its interpretation by another author. Traditionally, the task of the translator was understood as that of an invisible medium communicating between discrete and distinct linguistic worlds. Yet contemporary theorists have criticised this imperative for encouraging the invisibility of translation work (Venuti 1995), while advocating for transparency in translation (Benjamin 2002, 260).

The conventional view that valued above all the 'fidelity' of translation, demanding that the translation process be rendered invisible, was also challenged by the feminist school of translation (e.g. von Flotow 1997). Feminist translators sought to make the practice of translation not only visible but also to make it work for the feminist agenda, contesting understandings of translation work as a form of feminine reproductive labour viewed as subservient to the labour of the 'writer' (Wu 2013). Through the use of translation strategies such as supplementing, prefacing, footnoting, and even 'hijacking' of the original text, feminist translators proclaimed an 'anti-traditional, aggressive and creative approach to translation' (von Flotow 1991, 70).

Queer translation theory and practice present sentiments similar to feminist approaches. Much like gender itself, translation is seen as a 'performative practice' rather than a direct reflection of the meaning in the original (Epstein and Gillett 2017, 1). The process of translation is an apt metaphor for queerness: forever oscillating between binaries (fidelity/infidelity, source/copy, original/interpretation), making the familiar strange and complicated, thus revealing the constructed and contingent nature of language, which is normally understood as solid, eternal, and 'natural' (Epstein and Gillett 2017, 1).

Translation is always a particular re-writing of an original text serving specific ideological and political purposes. A translation may constitute a political intervention, an attempt to re-signify familiar concepts through alternative interpretations of particular words, and/or to introduce new ways of thinking and talking about certain subjects. Translators have real agency and translations and are, therefore, significant cultural products in and of themselves, and not mere derivatives (Tymoczko 2010). If any translation means manipulating a text in the service of some power or ideology, then it may also serve an emancipatory agenda of gender and sexual activists. How, then can we translate 'queer' into Kyrgyzstani Russian?

This chapter is organised into three sections. First, I provide the essential background to Kyrgyzstani society and politics with a focus on LGBT issues. Second, I examine the various meanings of 'queer', and the debates that arose with its use in the post-Soviet space. Finally, I compare the two translations of *Queer Nation Manifesto* by ACT UP (1990) to show how competing approaches interpret the 'queer' in post-Soviet space.

Background: Being LGBT in Kyrgyzstan

Non-heterosexual and gender non-conforming people in Kyrgyzstan mostly refer to themselves and others in the community as *tema* (Russian, literally 'theme'). This code-word means people 'in the know' or those with insider knowledge, suggesting secrecy and privacy of identity, and by implication, its apolitical nature. Unlike in the English-speaking world, the tradition of appropriation of homophobic slurs as positive self-designations to be used by LGBT people with both irony and pride does not exist in Kyrgyzstan. The term 'LGBT', associated with transnational activism, started to be used in the early 2000s by some young non-heterosexual and transgender Kyrgyzstanis as a 'neutral' term to manage stigma and become 'sexual citizens', transforming private issues of gender identity and sexuality into political matters (Wilkinson and Kirey 2010). Yet more recently, the term 'LGBT' gained negative connotations through its association with foreign actors and agendas in the post-Soviet space. There is a third term that co-exists with the colloquial *tema* and the activist 'LGBT': *kvir*. Borrowed from the English 'queer', this relatively new term is used mostly within scholarly circles and those associated with contemporary art. I argue that *kvir* is not merely a loan translation, but a term utilised self-consciously and strategically in post-Soviet space as a radical alternative to both mainstream LGBT identity politics and the general conservative turn in society.

Kyrgyzstan's politics of gender and sexuality resonate with global trends and contradictions, especially the politics of translation (understood literally and figuratively), homonationalism and international conservative and neoliberal politics. The small state is influenced by agendas of global politics, such as population control policies, equal marriage debates, HIV and AIDS prevention efforts, development agencies' goals and funding opportunities that shape the conversations and infrastructure of local activism (Hoare 2016). Yet there are also some distinguishing features of LGBT politics that are rooted in Kyrgyzstan's Soviet past.

In the Soviet Union, after a brief period of radical liberalisation of sexuality following the October Revolution, male homosexuality was re-criminalised in European republics in 1934 (Healey 2001, 222). Anti-sodomy laws were introduced across Central Asia even earlier in the late 1920s. They were aimed at eradicating 'crimes constituting survivals of primitive custom' along with polygamy and paying the bride price (Healey 2001, 159). Sexual exploitation of boy-dancers (*bacha bozi* in Uzbek), as well as consensual adult same-sex practices (*muzhelozhestvo* in Russian and *besoqolbozlik* in Uzbek) were deemed 'backward' and at odds with the Soviet emancipation agenda for the 'oppressed peoples of the Orient' (Healey 2001, 160). Female homosexuality was not criminalised, but pathologised within medical discourse (Sarajeva 2001, Stella 2015). Thus, for much of the Soviet period homosexuality was designated as belonging either in prison or in a psychiatric ward. Homosexuality re-entered public discussion during the late perestroika years with the policy of *glasnost.* It was already the late 1980s when the first LGBT-themed publications and organisations appeared in the European republics of the Soviet Union (Healey 2017).

Kyrgyzstan became independent following the dissolution of the Soviet Union in 1991. Unlike other Central Asian countries, the Kyrgyz Republic has become known for a vibrant civil society and dynamic political life. Kyrgyzstan's early activism started with the creation of organisations dealing with HIV and AIDS. The country's two largest cities, Bishkek and Osh, both had vibrant gay scenes, with queer clubs frequented and patronised by straight celebrities, members of the police and even orthodox priests. According to the account of Vladimir Tiupin, the founder of the first Kyrgyz gay organisation, Oasis, the 1990s were a period of hitherto unseen liberation and openness for gay and lesbian communities. Despite this seeming liberalisation, Oasis was registered as a 'youth' organisation in 1995 – three years before male homosexuality was decriminalised in Kyrgyzstan (Kazybekov 2013).

Thanks to a political landscape that became increasingly liberal, several LGBT rights NGOs were officially registered in the early 2000s. Labrys, an organisation founded by lesbians and trans people in 2004, was initially registered as a 'women's organisation' in 2006, and was then re-registered as an LGBT rights organisation in 2010. Yet, LGBT activism and existence remain fraught. With a conservative turn in the region and in global politics since the mid-2000s, the 'live and let live' attitude to homosexuality prevalent in the 1990s has been replaced with discourses of traditional values and the preservation of the nation (Wilkinson and Kirey 2010; Boemcken, Boboyorov, and Bagdasarova 2018). Against this backdrop, many LGBT people and activists face homophobic discrimination and violence in Kyrgyzstan as part of a broader similar trend in other parts of the world.

In 2014 conservative members of the Kyrgyz parliament, Kurmanbek Diykanabev and Torobai Zulpukarov of the ruling Social Democratic Party of

Kyrgyzstan (SDPK) party, initiated a bill "On introducing amendments to some legal acts of the Kyrgyz Republic", otherwise known as the law on 'gay propaganda' (*Labrys.kg*, 22 June 2017). The proposed bill aimed to make it an administrative and a criminal offence to 'engage in propaganda of non-traditional sexual relations'. As of January 2018, the bill was still under revision in the Kyrgyz parliament in its second reading.

The text of the proposed bill was lifted verbatim from a law adopted in the Russian Federation in 2013. The European Human Rights Court ruled in June 2017 that the Russian ban on propaganda of 'non-traditional sexual relations among children' was discriminatory and limited the right to freedom of speech (Rankin 2017). Moreover, a recent study by the Centre for Independent Social Research demonstrates that the number of violent hate crimes against LGBT people in Russia has risen dramatically since the law was adopted (Kondakov 2017). When the state criminalised positive or even neutral representation of LGBT lives and relationships, it gave a licence to discriminate against this group of people. The Kyrgyz draft bill does not limit the ban to 'propaganda' among children, but outlaws any discussion of homosexuality and LGBT rights work. Activists and LGBT allies in Kyrgyzstan also claim that the number of homophobic attacks has increased drastically since the draft law was introduced in parliament and that the general public discourse in the media has become visibly hostile.

Although the draft law remains under consideration in Kyrgyzstan, violence against non-heterosexual and gender non-conforming people is on the rise. In fact, LGBT organisations and activists have come under attack since the draft law was introduced (*Labrys.kg,* 19 May 2015). For instance, in April 2015, unknown persons threw Molotov cocktails over the fence into the courtyard of the office of the LGBT organisation Labrys (*Labrys.kg*, 10 April 2015). On May 17th of that same year, nationalist vigilante groups Kalys and Kyrk Choro attacked a private event dedicated to the International Day Against Homophobia, Transphobia and Biphobia (IDAHOT) in Bishkek, the capital, by climbing over the fence, kicking in the lock of the gate and physically assaulting a young woman (*Labrys.kg*, 19 May 2015). LGBT people were also subjected to violent assaults when leaving Bishkek's only queer club. Many more cases of violence, harassment, blackmail and extortion, rape, death threats, police brutality, and torture are known to activist groups. Many more remain unreported (HRW 2014).

Non-heterosexual and gender non-conforming people face grave and urgent challenges in Kyrgyzstan. Debates on semantics and critiques of the dominant activist discourse may seem trivial and even counter-productive. Yet I argue that the discussion regarding the adoption of the word *kvir* is key to understanding the present and future of gender and sexual politics in Kyrgyzstan and worldwide.

Queer, *Kvir* and their Discontents

Like many words in English, 'queer' can be used as several parts of speech – as an adjective, a noun and a verb. As an adjective it means 'strange' or 'odd', referring to all things 'differing in some odd way from what is usual or normal' (Merriam-Webster Online Dictionary). 'Queer' in this sense designates a quality of departure from the perceived norm.

As a noun, the word 'queer' today is an example of a practice of linguistic appropriation used as a means of resistance against violence by oppressed groups. Originally used as a homophobic slur to refer primarily to homosexual men, this word started being used by non-heterosexual people more generally for self-identification, self-affirmation, and self-advocacy. In the 1990 *Queer Nation Manifesto*, written by a radical group of New York gays and lesbians called AIDS Coalition to Unleash Power (ACT UP), 'queer' is articulated (and subsequently translated) interestingly:

> Queer! Ah, do we really have to use that word? It's trouble. Every gay person has his or her own take on it. For some it means strange and eccentric and kind of mysterious. That's okay; we like that. But some gay girls and boys don't. They think they're more normal than strange. And for others "queer" conjures up those awful memories of adolescent suffering. Queer. It's forcibly bittersweet and quaint at best – weakening and painful at worst. Couldn't we just use "gay" instead? It's a much brighter word. And isn't it synonymous with "happy"? When will you militants grow up and get over the novelty of being different? Why Queer ... Well, yes, "gay" is great. It has its place. But when a lot of lesbians and gay men wake up in the morning we feel angry and disgusted, not gay. So we've chosen to call ourselves queer. Using "queer" is a way of reminding us how we are perceived by the rest of the world. It's a way of telling ourselves we don't have to be witty and charming people who keep our lives discreet and marginalised in the straight world. We use queer as gay men loving lesbians and lesbians loving being queer. Queer, unlike *gay*, doesn't mean *male*. And when spoken to other gays and lesbians it's a way of suggesting we close ranks, and forget (temporarily) our individual differences because we face a more insidious common enemy. Yeah, *queer* can be a rough word but it is

also a sly and ironic weapon we can steal from the homophobe's hands and use against him (Queer Nation Manifesto,
ACT UP, 1990) *[all original emphases]*.

In the English language and among LGBT+ activists, the term 'queer' has
come to be used as a more compact synonym to the ever-expanding
abbreviation designating the diversity of the community (the LGBT+). Some
people also choose to identify themselves as queer because they find it
impossible to identify with traditional labels for gender and sexuality such as
'gay' or 'female'. In this sense, the term 'queer' is consciously gender-neutral
and inclusive.

The word 'queer' can additionally be used as a verb. To queer something
means to 'spoil' or to 'ruin' it (Merriam-Webster Online Dictionary). This is the
way the word is most commonly used by critical scholars, who are collectively
called the school of 'queer theory'. Scholars like Judith Butler and Eve
Kosofky Sedgwick 'queer' conventional categories for talking about gender
and sexuality. Such queering is not exclusive to the fields of gender and
sexuality studies. Queer optics have been applied in spheres as diverse as
ecology, politics, and international relations (Mortimer-Sandilands and
Erickson 2010; Weber 2016).

By emphasising 'queer' as something that one *does* rather than something
one *is*, we can resolve a seeming paradox of 'queerness': whether it is based
on one's identity or affinity. When identities are queered, a worry arises that
the subsequent loss of differences (for identity is always articulated in relation
with and opposition to the other) will render the oppressed groups invisible
and further oppressed. Thus, many LGBT activists and feminists feel ill at
ease with queering, and have debated the concept of *kvir* in the post-Soviet
space (Sozaev 2015a and 2015b; Kharitonova 2014).

Despite the international popularity of the word 'queer', and its Russian
rendition – *kvir*, its meaning remains vague because it is so all-
encompassing, and some activists in post-Soviet countries have contested
this 'empty signifier' as a harmful negative term that 'needs to die' (Sozaev
2015a and 2015b). A discussion on whether Russian 'queer' is possible took
place within the post-Soviet Russian-speaking space in 2010 at a queer
festival in Saint Petersburg. The results of this discussion were published as
an edited volume on LGBT studies (Sozaev 2010). No definite answer is
given to the question posed in the title of the volume, yet a few misgivings are
voiced by several authors citing queer theory's foreign origins rooted in a
different historical and socio-political context, its elitism and incompre-
hensibility and its supposed apolitical nature (Sozaev 2010, 17). For instance,

Sergei Mozzhegorov calls to 'Forget Queer', arguing that the social constructivist approach behind queer theory when translated into activist practice is harmful for the LGBT movement (2010, 90). Similarly, Olga Gert (also known as Olgerta Kharitonova, the editor of the longest existing Russian-language lesbian feminist magazine Ostrov) writes that Russia is not ready to accept queer theory and politics due to their complexity and suggests that the social movements focus on feminism first (2010, 97).

Valerii Sozaev, a well-known Russian LGBT activist, points out that the concept of 'queer' has emerged out of a specific historical context of the gay and lesbian movement in the United States in the face of the AIDS epidemic of the 1980s and 1990s. 'What is the history of *kvir* in Russia? And does "queer" mean the same thing in the United States as *kvir* does in Russia? Is the performative power and the consequences of using the word *kvir* in Russian equivalent to the use of "queer" in English?', he asks (2015b). Sozaev asserts that the word *kvir* entered the Russian language through academic studies of gender and sexuality, as a euphemistic replacement of the potentially compromising word 'homosexuality'. It was thus hollowed out of all subversive and protest potential from its birth.

The word travelled into the LGBT activists' vocabulary as a convenient disguise to hide their homosexuality. Sozaev, for instance, narrates an anecdote of how LGBT activists decided on the name *Kvir Fest* for a festival in Saint Petersburg in 2008/2009. They wanted to organise an event that would attract the right audience, but would not give rise to unwanted attention from authorities and homophobes. Since the word *kvir* was virtually unknown to anyone outside the community, it was chosen as the 'safest' word. Sozaev (2015a) feels that *kvir* is hostile to both lesbian feminism and gay male liberation because it prevents the politicisation of LGBT communities around their identities as oppressed groups. As such, he argues, it is destructive for the movement and the community and detrimental to 'gay pride', because, according to *kvir*, there is no such thing as 'gay' (Sozaev 2015a).

In Sozaev's and Kharitonova's objections to *kvir* we can discern their doubts regarding the word's emancipatory potential. They both object to the label as a noun (as a way of labelling oneself and as a set of substantial philosophical ideas). I contend that this contradiction can be resolved if we think of 'queer' as a verb. Queering categories does have an emancipatory effect. Rather than erasing oppressed identities, it queers them, makes them ambiguous, complex, multidimensional and intersectional. Queering identities creates grounds for solidarity and coalition building based on affinity, not complete identity with another human/non-human being.

Translating 'Queer' into Russian: The Story of One Manifesto

Queer Nation Manifesto, originally distributed at the 1990 Gay Pride parade in New York by ACT UP, is a historical text of the LGBT movement. This inflammatory text was created against the backdrop of a raging AIDS epidemic and the homophobic policy of neglect by the United States government. The manifesto expressed a sense of urgency, desperation, and defiance with statements like 'I hate straights!' (ACT UP 1990). *Queer Nation Manifesto* sparked a short-lived, but extremely effective and influential political campaign, with chapters all across the USA (Stryker 2015). This text marks a turning point in LGBT politics in the US and globally.

Two recent translations of this text into Russian illustrate the competing visions of the meanings and uses of 'queer' in post-Soviet space. The manifesto was only translated into Russian in 2016 when two groups decided to translate it independently of each other. The first translation was mine, and appeared in the Bishkek-based queer feminist zine (self-published magazine with small circulation) *Weird Sisters*, edited by Oksana Shatalova (2016). The issue was dedicated to Queer feminism and built on a debate taking place between our group and a feminist group in Kazakhstan (Kazfem), that publishes a feminist zine called *Yudol*. *Weird Sisters* collective first responded to an article published in *Yudol* (2016) which argued that human sexuality is predetermined by biological factors, such as exposure to certain hormones while in utero, and is therefore inborn (Aprel'skaia 2016, 34). Our group responded with a polemical text entitled 'Heterosexual in the womb, or constructivists' response to essentialists', questioning the need to appeal to 'nature' that even the most progressive social justice movements succumb to at times (*Weird Sisters* 2016). We then dedicated the following issue to 'queering feminism' and titled it 'Nature Won't Stop the Queer!' (Priroda kviru ne pomekha!). This issue contained two translations of feminist and queer activist classics – *The Transfeminist Manifesto* by Emi Koyama (2001) translated by Maria Vilkovisky and edited by Ruth Jenrbekova (Creole Centre, Kazakhstan) and *Queer Nation Manifesto* (1990) translated by me.

The decision to translate the text of *Queer Nation Manifesto* was contextual to the discussions taking place within/across the Central Asian feminist and LGBT activists' communities. Translation in this case was a significant intervention to introduce a cultural change. This translation is a record of ideological contestation. 'Queering' gender and sexuality, and even the idea of 'nature' itself, was our answer to essentialist tendencies within the community of activists around us.

I translated the title of the *Manifesto* as 'Manifest kvir-naroda', meaning,

Manifesto of Queer People. Consistent with how we previously used the word *kvir* in our projects, I chose to use *kvir* to translate 'queer' in most of the text. In some cases, however, I used *izvrashchenets* ('pervert', masculine) and/or *izvrashchenka* (feminine). Nouns in the Russian language have three genders (masculine, feminine, and neutral). Therefore, it was a challenge to find one single word that would include both feminine and masculine-identifying individuals as well as those who identify with both/neither. Discussions among Russian-speaking feminists on the use of feminitives and gender-neutral/ inclusive language have produced a number of now widely used forms. For instance, using punctuation, one can write *izvrashchen_ka/ets* to include both genders and allow for the possibility of neither – the underscore sign signifying the tentativeness of gender – which is what I did. Also, when translating, I used both masculine and feminine first-person gender to convey two voices that I detected in the Manifesto – one of a gay man and another of a lesbian woman. The transition between two voices in the text is not clearly marked thus producing a queering effect.

The other translation of *Queer Nation Manifesto* into Russian was undertaken by Gulnara Kurmanova, an activist based in Bishkek. Published in December 2016 on the website of the Russian initiative group *Deistviie*. A commentary to the publication attributes the original idea to translate the text to Sozaev – the very person who previously advocated death for the concept of *kvir*. The Manifesto title appears in this translation as *Manifest Natsii Pidarov*. Here 'queer' is replaced with the Russian homophobic slur for a male homosexual man – *pidar*. An explanation from Sozaev follows:

> It is our conscious decision to use *pidar* instead of *kvir* in the Russian translation, because we think that the extrapolation of the largely unknown to the wider public English word 'queer' will reduce the deconstructive potential of the text. Moreover, there is a tendency in the Russian language to use the word *kvir* in the meaning of 'genderqueer', that is why we strove to avoid such confusion. However, the difficulty with replacing the word *kvir* with *pidar* is also in the fact that the English word is gender-neutral and its use was initiated among other considerations in order to avoid the androcentric 'gay', which the authors of the manifesto discuss. Unfortunately, despite all our attempts to find an adequate equivalent for a gender-neutral word in Russian, we did not succeed. We decided not to use the word *izvrashchentsi* (perverts), because it does not carry the emphasis on sexuality, which is important when translating the word 'queer' (forward to Kurmanova's translation by Sinel'nikov and Sozaev).

The choice of *pidar* as a more subversive and deconstructive equivalent to 'queer' in Russian rings true to the original intention in ACT UP's Manifesto: 'Using "queer" is a way of reminding us how we are perceived by the rest of the world' (ACT UP 1990). After all, as Valerii Sozaev rightly pointed out, when someone is attacked on homophobic grounds, the bashers are not likely to shout '*Kvir!*', but homophobic slurs like *pedik* (fag), *pidaras* (pederast), *gomik* (homo), *lezbukha* (lesbo) (Sozaev 2015b). Yet, when choosing *pidar*, the authors of the translation also pick one particular story of queer experience (that of a gay man) and universalise it.

What is remarkable in this story is that the *Deistviie* initiative group translated *Queer Nation Manifesto* into Russian despite Sozaev's aversion to the term, which he had openly voiced (2010, 2015a, and 2015b). Could this be interpreted as an LGBT activist's attempt at 'hijacking' *kvir* and appropriating it for his struggle in the form that feels authentic and politically productive? Some activists' anxiety regarding 'foreign' concepts as inauthentic, imposed, or even colonising is quite understandable and justified. Yet this anxiety about using *kvir* in a post-Soviet context is based on the traditional understanding of language and translation. Within this paradigm, language is seen as separate and corresponding to reality, while a translation seeks to match that correspondence perfectly in another language.

Conclusion

I contend that we need to think of the use and translation of 'queer' in the Wittgensteinian sense of 'language games' (2009). By this, I mean his idea that concepts do not need to be clearly defined to be meaningful. His analogy between a language and a game demonstrates that words have meaning depending on the uses made of them in the various and multiform activities of human life. The multiple uses of 'queer' across languages bear a 'family resemblance', but are not in a relationship of one-to-one correspondence of equivalence and identity. Each utterance and translation of 'queer' hides a particular story of political and ideological resistance and struggle.

While some part of LGBT and feminist activists in Kyrgyzstan have embraced *kvir* and queering as a practice of resistance, the concept still remains confusing for many in the community/ies. So, to rerun our opening question, can 'queer' be translated into Kyrgyzstani Russian? I must confess: the answer is that it has been and will continue to be translated in multiple ways and there can be no one 'correct' translation.

References

Aprel'skaia, Mariana. 2016. "Igra gormonov: seksual'naiia orientatsiia skvoz' prizmu essentsialistskogo i konstruktivistskogo podkhodov." [The Game of Hormones: sexual orientation through the prism of essentialist and constructivist approaches] *Yudol* 2: 31–35. https://yadi.sk/i/Qp-xjshBr7rCn.

Benjamin, Walter. 2002. "The task of the translator." in *Selected Writings, Volume 1, 1913–1926*, edited by Bullock, Marcus and Michael W. Jennings, 253–265. Cambridge, UK: The Belknap Press of Harvard University Press.

Boemcken, Marc von, Hafiz Boboyorov and Nina Bagdasarova. 2018. "Living dangerously: securityscapes of Lyuli and LGBT people in urban spaces of Kyrgyzstan", *Central Asian Survey* 37 (1): 68–84.

Epstein, B.J. and Robert Gillett. 2017. *Queer in Translation*. New York, NY: Routledge.

Healey, Dan. 2001. *Homosexual desire in revolutionary Russia: The regulation of sexual and gender dissent.* Chicago, IL: University of Chicago Press.

Healey, Dan. 2017. *Russian homophobia from Stalin to Sochi*. London, UK: Bloomsbury.

Hoare, Joanna Pares. 2016. "Doing gender activism in a donor-organised framework: constraints and opportunities in Kyrgyzstan." *Nationalities Papers* 44 (2): 281–298.

Kazybekov, Eldos. 2013. "Interviu: Pervii gei-aktivist Kirgizstana" [Interview: The first gay activist of Kyrgyzstan], *Kloop*, 5 February, 2013. https://kloop.kg/blog/2013/02/05/interv-yu-pervy-j-gej-aktivist-ky-rgy-zstana/.

Kharitonova, Olgerta. 2014. "Kvir kak otritsaniie." [Queer as a negation] In *Kvir-seksual'nost': politiki i praktiki* [Queer sexualities: politics and practices], edited by Irina Solomatina and Tatiana Shchurko, 21–24. Minsk, Belarus: Galiiafy.

Kondakov, Aleksandr. 2017. *Prestupleniia na pochve nenavisti protiv LGBT v Rossii* [Hate crimes against LGBT in Russia]. St Petersburg, Russia: Centre for Independent Social Research Renome.

Koyama, Emi. 2001. "The Transfeminist Manifesto." In *Catching A Wave: Reclaiming Feminism for the Twenty-First Century*, edited by Rory Dicker and Alison Piepmeier. Boston, MA: Northeastern University Press.

Kurmanova, Gulnara. 2016. "Manifest natsii pidarov." [Queer Nation Manifesto] *Deistvie*, 2 December. http://center-action.org/2016/02/12/ manifest-natsii-pidarov-queer-nation/.

Labrys. 2015a. "Kirgizstan: bezopasnost' LGBTIQ-pravozashchitnikov pod ugrozoi." [Kyrgyzstan: safety of the LGBTIQ rights activists is in danger] *Labrys.kg*, April 10. http://labrys.kg/ru/news/full/682.html.

Labrys. 2015b. "Sryv LGBT-pravozashchitnogo meropriiatiia: Khronika." [Disruption of an LGBT-rights event: a chronology] *Labrys.kg*, May 19. http:// labrys.kg/ru/news/full/685.html.

Labrys. 2017. "Zametka o diskriminatsionnom zakonoproekte v Kyrgyzstane" [A note regarding the discriminatory draft law in Kyrgyzstan] *Labrys.kg*, 22 June. http://labrys.kg/ru/news/full/699.html.

Mortimer-Sandilands, Catriona and Bruce Ericson, eds. 2010. *Queer Ecologies: Sex, Nature, Politics, Desire*. Indianapolis, IN: Indiana University Press, 2010.

Rankin, Jennifer. 2017. "Russian 'gay propaganda' law ruled discriminatory by the European court." *The Guardian*. 20 June.

Sarajeva, K. 2001. *Lesbian Lives: Sexuality, Space and Subculture in Moscow*. Stockholm, Sweden: Acta Universitatis Stockholmiensis.

Sozaev, Valerii, ed. 2010. *Vozmozhen li "kvir" po-russki? LGBTK issledovaniia. Mezhdistsiplinarnii sbornik*. [Is Russian 'queer' possible? LGBTQ studies. An interdisciplinary collection of texts] Saint Petersburg, Russia: Coming Out/Vykhod.

Sozaev, Valerii. 2015a. "Kvir dolzhen umeret." ['Queer' must die] *OutLoud Magazine*, May 1. http://outloudmag.eu/events/item/kvir-dolzhen-umeret.

Sozaev, Valerii. 2015b. "Skromnoie obaianiie kvir, ili kvir kak illiuziia." [Modest charm of the queer, or queer as an illusion]. *Makeout*, November 23. https:// makeout.by/2015/11/23/skromnoe-obayanie-kvir-ili-kvir-kak-illyuziya.html.

Spivak, Gayatri. 2007. "Translation as culture". *In Translation: Reflections, Refractions, Transformations*, edited by Paul St-Pierre and Prafulla C. Kar, 263–276. Amsterdam, Netherlands: John Benjamins Publishing Company.

Stella, Francesca. 2015. *Lesbian Lives in Soviet and post-Soviet Russia. Post/Socialism and Gender Sexualities.* Basingstoke, UK: Palgrave Macmillan.

Stryker, Susan. 2015. "Queer Nation". *LGBTQ Encyclopaedia*. http://www. glbtqarchive.com/ssh/queer_nation_S.pdf .

Suyarkulova, Mohira, trans. 2016. "ACT UP, Manifest kvir-naroda" [Queer Nation Manifesto], *Weird Sisters* 5: 49–69. Bishkek, Kyrgyzstan: STAB.

Suyarkulova, Mohira, trans. Adrienne Rich. 2014. *"Obiazatel'naia geteroseksual'nost' i lesbiiskoie sushchestvovaniie."* [Compulsory heterosexuality and lesbian existence], *Kvir-issledovaniia* 1. Bishkek, Kyrgyzstan: STAB. http://www.art-initiatives.org/ru/content/obyazatelnaya-geteroseksualnost-i.

Suyarkulova, Mohira, trans. 2013. *Queer Communism Manifesto.* Bishkek, Kyrgyzstan: STAB. http://en.art-initiatives.org/?page_id=6830.

Tymoczko, Maria, ed. 2010. *Translation, Resistance, Activism. Essays on the role of translators as agents of change.* Boston, MA: University of Massachusetts Press.

Venuti, Lawrence. 1995. *The Translator's Invisibility: A history of translation.* London, UK: Routledge.

von Flotow, Luise. 1991. "Feminist Translation: Contexts, Practices and Theories." *TTR : traduction, terminologie, redaction* 4, 2: 69–84.

Von Flotow, Luise. 1997. *Translation and Gender: Translating in the 'Era of Feminism'.* Manchester, UK: St Jerome Publishing.

Weber, Cynthia. 2016. *Queer International Relations: Sovereignty, Sexuality and the Will to Knowledge.* Oxford, UK: Oxford University Press.

Weird Sisters. 2016. "Geteroseksual v utrobe, ili otvet konstruktivistok essentsialistkam." [Heterosexual in the womb, or constructivists' response to essentialists] *STAB*, 26 April http://www.art-initiatives.org/ru/content/geteroseksual-v-utrobe-ili-otvet.

Wilkinson, Cai and Anna Kirey. 2010. "What's in a name? The personal and political meanings of 'LGBT' for non-heterosexual and transgender youth in Kyrgyzstan." *Central Asian Survey* 29 (4): 485–499.

Wittgenstein, Ludwig. 2009. *Philosophical Investigations,* 4th edition, edited by P.M.S. Hacker and Joachim Schulte. Hoboken, NJ: Wiley-Blackwell.

Wu, E-chou. 2013. "Feminist Translation/Feminist Adaptation. Ang Lee's *Sense and Sensibility.*" Paper presented at the ACSIS conference "On the Move", 11–13 June, Norrkoping, Sweden. http://www.ep.liu.se/ecp/095/003/ecp13095003.pdf .

4

Indigenous Sexualities: Resisting Conquest and Translation

MANUELA L. PICQ AND JOSI TIKUNA

Sexual diversity has historically been the norm, not the exception, among Indigenous peoples. Ancestral tongues prove it. In Juchitán, Mexico, *muxes* are neither man nor woman, but a Zapotec gender hybridity. In Hawai'i, the *māhū* embrace both the feminine and masculine. The Māori term *takatāpui* describes same-sex intimate friendships, and since the 1980s it is the term used alongside the term queer. Non-monogamy is the norm among the Zo'é peoples in Amazonia and in the Ladakhis in the Himalayas. In other words, Indigenous sexualities were never straight: ranging from cross-dressing to homo-affective families, they are as diverse as the peoples who practice them. But if native terminologies referring to same-sex practices and non-binary, fluid understandings of gender existed before the emergence of LGBT frameworks, why are Indigenous experiences invisible in international sexual rights debates?

Language shows that Indigenous queerness, in its own contextual realities, predates the global LGBT framework. Yet Indigenous experiences are rarely perceived as a locus of sexual diversity. This is partly because Indigenous peoples are imagined as remnants of the past, whereas sexual diversity is associated with political modernity. In *Indians in Unexpected Places*, Phillip Deloria (2004) explored cultural expectations that branded Indigenous peoples as having missed out on modernity. Sexual freedoms, in turn, are associated with global human rights, secular modernity, and Western cosmopolitanism (Rahman 2014; Scott 2018). Indigenous homosexualities provoke chuckles because they disrupt expectations of modernity. They surprise because they express sexual diversity in non-modern places.

Illustrations by Laura Bensoussan. Reproduced with permission

Indigenous queerness is also invisible because sexual terminologies are lost in translation. The meanings of gender roles and sexual practices are cultural constructions that inevitably get lost when they are decontextualised in cultural (and linguistic) translation. The spectrum of Indigenous sexualities does not fit the confined Western registries of gender binaries, heterosexuality, or LGBT codification. It is not these idioms that are untranslatable, but rather the cultural and political fabric they represent. Indigenous sexualities defy contemporary LGBT and queer frameworks.

Queer debates do not travel well, whether in space or in time. The idea that a person is homosexual, for instance, stems from contemporary assumptions of sexual identity and is only possible after the invention of homosexuality (Katz 2007). Mark Rifkin (2011) asks when Indian became straight because heterosexual vocabulary is as inappropriate to understand Indigenous worldviews as the binary imagination. The problem is not only that the global sexual rights regime cannot account for the place of desire in pre-colonial societies; it is also that discussions of Indigenous sexualities in English risk being anachronistic and misrepresentative. Indigenous sexualities are embedded in the impossibilities of epistemological translation.

This chapter sheds light on the value of Indigenous diversities for non-Indigenous worlds. There are an estimated 370 million Indigenous persons in 90 countries; over 5000 nations that speak thousands of languages. Indigenous peoples are as diverse as the processes of colonisation they continue to endure. There are many terms to refer to them – Indian, Native, First Nations, Indigenous, and Tribal peoples – because their experiences relate to a plurality of power relations that vary across colonial experiences.[1] The term 'Indian' was invented by colonial governments to subordinate vastly distinct peoples in a homogenising legal status (Van Deusen 2015). Indigenousness is a political identity. It refers less to a constitutive who/what than to the otherness implied by it. Mohawk and Cherokee scholars Taiaiake Alfred and Jeff Corntassel (2005) define being Indigenous today as an oppositional identity linked to the consciousness of struggle against ongoing forms of dispossession and assimilation by subtler forms of colonialism that spread out of Europe. This includes sexual colonisation. As colonial powers appropriated Indigenous territories, they tried to control, repress and erase Indigenous sexualities. Colonisation regulated Indigenous gender experiences, supplanting them with Western sexual codes associated with (Christian) modernity. Scholars exposed the heteronormativity of colonialism (Smith 2010), insisted on the value to decolonise queer studies and queer decolonial studies (Driskill et al. 2011; Morgensen 2011). We contribute a linguistic perspective to this debate.

Indigenous sexualities resist translation as much as they resist erasure. This essay first looks at the vast diversity of Indigenous sexualities across time and borders through language. We then show how Tikuna women are resisting ongoing forms of sexual colonisation in Amazonia, revealing the

---

[1]   Official definitions have varied over time as states manipulate legislation, blood quantum, and census depending on their interest to erase, regulate, or displace Indigenous presence (Kauanui 2008). If Indigenous belonging is contested in the Americas, the concept is even fuzzier in regions that did not experience large European settler immigration, like Asia (Baird 2016).

ways the decolonisation of sexualities is central to Indigenous self-determination.

Lost in Colonial Translation

Indigenous sexualities defy LGBT categorisation; they resist translation into the conceptual limits of LGBT categories. Juchitán, internationally depicted as a gay paradise, is known for having gender freedoms in stark contrast with the rest of Mexico. Their Zapotec society recognises *muxes* as a third gender (Mirandé 2017, 15). The *muxes* are people who are biologically male but embody a third gender that is neither male nor female, and who refuse to be translated as transvestite. *Muxes* were traditionally seen as a blessing from the gods; today they remain an integral part of society.

Muxes cannot be reduced to LGBT categorisation, nor can their experience be exported or replicated elsewhere. They are better approached from queer understandings of sexuality as fluid. Elders say that in ancient, pre-colonial Zapotec language there was no difference when referring to a man or a woman; there were no genders. In ancient Zapotec, *la-ave* referred to people, *la-ame* to animals, and *la-ani* to inanimate beings. There was no he or she (Olita 2017). This changed with the arrival of the Spanish conquistadores who introduced the feminine and masculine genders. How are we to translate *muxes* in languages that are structured around gender? The *muxes* are just one example of many sexual registries that were lost in colonial translation.

Celebrations of non-heteronormative sexualities abounded before the arrival of Europeans in 1492. Same-sex relations were celebrated in Moche pottery (AD 15–800), along the northern Pacific coast of contemporary Peru. Moche stirrup spout vessels depict a variety of sexual acts but rarely vaginal penetration, emphasising male genitalia and the movement of fluids between bodies as a form of communication (Weismantel 2004). In the Pacific islands, Māori carvings celebrated same-sex and multiple relationships (Te Awekotuku 2003). In the Andes, the Inkas summoned a queer figure called *chuqui chinchay* to mediate a political crisis in the late fifteenth century (Horswell 2005). The *chuqui chinchay,* a revered figure in Andean culture, was the mountain deity of the jaguars. It was also the patron of dual-gendered peoples, who acted as shamans in Andean ceremonies. These *quariwarmi* (man-woman) cross-dressed to mediate the dualism of Andean cosmology, performing rituals that involved same-sex erotic practices. They embodied a third creative force between the masculine and the feminine in Andean philosophy.

Colonisers had a hard time recognising native sexualities for what they were.

Colonial chronicles from the sixteenth century to the eighteenth century described non-binary sexualities, telling of genders they could not comprehend (or accept). Will Roscoe (1998, 12–15) gathered colonial documents reporting such accounts. French expeditions in Florida described 'hermaphrodites' among the Timucua Indians as early as 1564. Colonial engravings depict them as warriors, hunters, and weavers. In the Mississippi Valley, French colonisers reported a third gender, called *ikoueta* in Algonkian language, males who adopted gender roles. They went to war, sang in ceremonies, and participated in councils. According to colonial reports, they were holy, and nothing could be decided without their advice. Another French coloniser, Dumont de Montigny, described males that did women's work and had sex with men among the Natchez in the lower Mississippi region in the eighteenth century. In what is now Texas, the Spanish Cabeza de Vaca reported men who dressed and lived like women. Even Russian traders in the sub-arctic region documented gender diversity among Native communities in what is today Alaska. Despite Russian efforts to suppress third genders, the Chugach and Koniag celebrated those they called 'two persons in one' and considered them lucky.

Linguistic registries show that indigenous peoples approached gender as a fluid affair before conquest and assimilation. Roscoe's linguistic index documents language for alternative genders in over 150 tribes in North America. Alternative genders existed among the Creek, Chickasaw, and Cherokee. In Navajo language, *nádleehí* means 'the changing one'. In Osage, Omaha, Kansa, and Oto languages, the term *mixu'ga* literally means "moon-instructed", referring to the distinct abilities and identity that the moon conferred them (Roscoe 1998, 13). Alternative genders were often associated with spiritual powers. The Potawatomi considered them extraordinary people. For the Lakota, *winkte* people had auspicious powers and could predict the future. Lakota warriors visited *winkte* before going to battle to increase their strength. The *he'emane'o* directed the important victory-dance because they embodied the central principles of balance and synthesis in Cheyenne philosophy (Roscoe 1998, 14).

Women engaged in same-sex practices and alternative genders that marked lifelong identities. Nearly a third of the groups in Roscoe's index had ways of referring specifically to women who undertook male roles. Evelyn Blackwood (1984) argues that the female cross-gender role in Native-American contexts constituted an opportunity to assume male roles permanently and to marry women. A trader for the American Fur Company that travelled up the Missouri River reported that Woman Chief, a Crow woman who led men into battle, had four wives and was a respected authority who sat in Crow councils (Roscoe 1998, 78).

Blackwood (1984, 35) argues that Native American ideology among Western tribes dissociated sexual behaviour from concepts of male/female gender roles and was not concerned with gender identity. This means for instance that gender roles did not restrict sexual partners – individuals had a gender identity but not a corresponding sexual identity. In other words, sex was not entangled in gender ideology. Blackwood stresses the unimportance of biological sex for gender roles in native worldviews for Western tribes in the US. There was much overlapping of masculine and feminine, and people who were once married and had kids would later in life pursue same-sex relationships. Roscoe (1998, 10) interprets this fluidity as a distinction between reproductive and non-reproductive sex rather than a distinction between heterosexual and same-sex sexuality. Interpretations vary. What is certain is that Indigenous cultures have long recognised non-heterosexual sexualities and alternative genders, socially respected, integrated, and often revered them.

Sexual Colonisation

This rich diversity in native sexualities took a hard hit with post-1492 colonial expansion, which brutally repressed non-heteronormative practices. Chronicles like the *Relación de Servicios en Indias* labelled Inka sacred figures like the *chuqui chinchay* as diabolical and described natives as 'ruinous people' who 'are all sodomites' – and called for their extermination (Horsewell 2005, 1–2). An infamous example is the 1513 massacre of 'sodomites' by Spanish conquistador Vasco Nunez de Balboa in Panama. Balboa threw the brother of Chief Quaraca and 40 of his companions to the dogs for being dressed as women. The brutal killings were engraved in Theodore de Bry's 1594 *Les Grands Voyages*. In another macabre episode, French colonisers tie a hermaphrodite to a cannon in northern Brazil. Capuchin priest Yves d'Evreux describes how the French chased the 'poor Indian' who was 'more man than a woman', and convicted him 'to purify the land' (Fernandes and Arisi 2017, 7). The punishment consisted of tying the person's waist to the mouth of the cannon and making a native chief light the fuse that dismantled the body in front of all other 'savages'.

Perhaps European colonisers could not understand native sexualities; they did not have the words to. They could not recognise sexualities differing from their own, and, generally, associated native sexualities with immoral, perverse, and unnatural sexualities. Vanita Seth (2010) explains the European difficulty in representing difference as stemming from a broader inability to translate the New World into a familiar language. In that sense, the 'discovery' was severely impaired by the colonisers' inability to convert what they encountered across the New World into accessible language. Yet the colonial destruction of native sexualities is more than a mere inability to see otherness. Labelling native sexualities as unnatural justified violent repression, and the heterosexualisation of Indians was as much a process of modernisation as of dispossession.

Estevão Fernandes and Barbara Arisi (2017) explain how the colonisation of native sexualities imposed a foreign configuration of family and intimate relations in Brazil. The state created bureaucratic structures to civilise the Indians. In the 1750s, the *Directory of Indians* established administrative control of intimacy and domesticity that restructured sex and gender in daily life. Bureaucratic interventions centred on compulsory heterosexuality, decrying the 'incivility' of Indigenous homes where 'several families (...) live as beasts not following the laws of honesty (...) due to the diversity of the sexes' (Fernandes and Arisi 2017, 32). Indigenous households were subject to the monogamous 'laws of honesty' and Indigenous heterosexualisation initiated the process of civilisation. Rifkin (2011, 9) refers to a similar process in Native North America as 'heterohomemaking'. Heteronormativity made it impossible for any other sexuality, gender, or family organising to exist. The framing of native sexualities as queer or straight impose the colonial state as the axiomatic unit of political collectivity. Indigenous peoples were forced to translate themselves in terms consistent with the state and its jurisdiction. Sexual codification related to racial boundaries defining access to or exclusion from citizenship and property rights (McClintock 1995).

The historical and linguistic archives are crucial even if they defy translation: they refer to social fabrics that have been largely disrupted, repressed, and destroyed. Each language brought a singular understanding of gender. Indigenous genders cannot be reduced to homo or trans sexuality. It would be an anachronism to translate pre-conquest realities into contemporary frames. In pre-conquest societies, third genders were not an anomaly or difference, but constitutive of a whole. Thus, debates on whether to approach native sexualities as berdache, two-spirit, or third genders miss the point. Native sexualities cannot be reduced to the addition of more genders to established sexual registries; they invoke complex social fabrics that are untranslatable in the limited framework of hetero/homosexuality. They invoked native epistemologies and worldviews beyond sexuality.

Centuries of sexual colonising erased non-Western Indigenous understandings of sexuality. But they are still there. During Brazil's National Meeting of Indigenous Students in 2017, a group discussed self-determination through issues ranging from land demarcation to LGBT issues. Tipuici Manoki said that homosexuality is taboo among Indian communities, 'but it exists'.[2] Today,

---

[2]   https://brasil.elpais.com/brasil/2018/02/01/politica/1517525218_900516.html?id_

Indigenous peoples often utilise the global sexual rights framework for self-representation and rights claims. In 2013, the Inter-American Commission on Human Rights of the Organisation of American States heard the testimonies of elected officials at a panel 'Situation of the Human Rights of Lesbian, Gay, Bisexual, Transgender and Intersex Indige-nous Persons in the Americas'. In the US, at least three tribes have formally recognised marriage equality for same-sex couples. Indigenous sexualities resisted conquest and genocide in their own ways, with words of their own, before and beyond the LGBT framework.

Sexual Resurgence in Amazonia

Resisting is exactly what Indigenous peoples are doing in Amazonia. Originary peoples in Amazonia have long had words to refer to non-heterosexual practice, and their languages may be considered queer by contemporary frameworks. In Tupinambá, *tibira* is a man who has sex with men and *çacoaimbeguira* is a woman who has sex with women. The documentary 'Tibira means gay' shows the variety of sexual identities in Indigenous communities. Other languages have words for queer practices: *cudinhos* in Guaicurus, *guaxu* in Mbya, *cunin* in Krahò, *kudina* in Kadiwéu, *hawakyni* in Javaé.

The Tikuna, one of the largest Indigenous groups in Amazonia, speak an isolate language.[3] In Tikuna, *Kaigüwecü* is the word that describes a man who has sex with another man; *Ngüe Tügümaêgüé* describes a woman who has sex with another woman. But these words were unrelated to the Rule of Nations, a central principle of Tikuna society that organises marriage among clans in rules of exogamy. In Tikuna philosophy, to marry well is to marry people from different clans: a member from the clan of the bird (ewi) can marry with a member from the clan of the jaguar (ai), but not a member of its own clan. Unions within a clan are considered incestuous, and therefore unforgivable. In short, Tikuna unions are legitimised along clan lines, not sex. Things started to change, however, with the recent arrival of evangelical missionaries, like the New Neopentacostal Churches, who introduced different expectations about marriage. Rather than worrying about clans, missionaries are concerned with sex, more specifically with regulating sexuality. These churches framed homo-affective relationships as sinful. Progressively, what were uneventful couples under clan lines became abnormal 'lesbian' couples in religious rhetoric. Forbidden love was displaced

[3]   A language isolate has no demonstrable genealogical relationship with other languages. Tikuna is a language isolate with no common ancestry with any other known language.

from within the clan to within one's gender.

Homo-affective Tikuna experiences vary. Some are marginalised by their communities, treated with contempt by their families or even expelled from their homes. Many fear making their sexuality public. 'Some mothers even forbid their daughters to see me because I am *machuda*'[4] said one of them. Discrimination turns into social marginalisation and destroys ties of cultural belonging, making women feel excluded. Some are forced to leave their homes and communities, even to suicide. In other cases, families and communities normalise sexual diversity. This happened to 32-year-old Waire'ena. Her father, a priest in a new Church called Brotherhood of Santa Cruz, was hesitant in accepting his daughter's sexuality because of the repercussions in the community. As a public religious-political figure, he worried about moral considerations like honour and respect that were elements used to negotiate his legitimacy and social position. He eventually talked to the head priest of his Church, who described the situation as a 'challenge from God'. That is when he 'woke up' tells Waire'ena. He interpreted the challenge to be teaching his followers the tolerance of diverse forms of sexuality as all being blessed by God. His mission became to convince his community to accept his daughter's homo-affective choices. He talked to people across his Church, preached for same-sex love, and countered homophobia in his community.

Tikuna women too are taking matters into their own hands, invoking the Rule of Nations to defend their autonomy to love in their own Tikuna terms. They defend homo-affective relationships as consistent with the clan rules of exogamy. For Botchicüna, there is little doubt that sexual diversity is intrinsically Indigenous; sexual discrimination was brought in by a vogue of evangelical religions. 'Our ancestors experienced people living homo-affective lives but never interpreted it as something malicious, it is religion that came to interfere with our culture trying to evangelise us'. Churches introduced lesbianism as a forbidden love, permeating Tikuna cosmovision with exogenous moralities that signal the colonial power of religion over Indigenous peoples. What is detrimental to Tikuna culture is the foreign imposition of religions by missionaries. Homo-affective ties, they claim, respect the Rule of Nations and therefore reinforce Tikuna self-determination.

Tikuna women are invoking ancestrality to battle new waves of homophobia introduced by outsiders. Their homo-affective families raise their children in accordance with ancestral clan lines. Women claim that same-sex relationships give continuity to Tikuna Rule of Nations, insisting on clan lines

---

4   Machuda, from macho, is a pejorative way to refer to women who have sex with women as masculine not feminine.

to secure sexual freedoms. In their experience, culture and sexual autonomy complement one another. Tikuna women are blending political registries, combining ancestral worldviews with current LGBT referents to defend sexual autonomy in their local contexts. In doing so, they are using sexual politics towards Indigenous resurgence. They negotiate current politics to define their world for themselves, reclaiming the past to shape their futures (Aspin and Hutchings 2007).

Are Tikuna societies modern because they permit homo-affective love? The stories of sexual diversity told above invite us to reconsider assumed cartographies of modernity. They debunk notions of natural peripheries isolated from global modernity and embedded in colonial processes. Amazonia is not that disentangled from global dynamics nor a land without (sexual) history. Similarly, narratives that posit sexual liberation as a Western, modern phenomenon need reframing (Rahman 2014). Their sexual politics are not about modernity and we should not invoke LGBT codification to validate them. Indigenous sexualities defy translation, they refer to political systems beyond frameworks of LGBT rights.

Conclusion

For many Indigenous peoples across the world, diverse sexualities and multiple genders are not a Western introduction. Heteronormativity is. Indigenous intimacies were repressed, pathologised and erased by violent processes of colonial dispossession. Yet Indigenous languages resist so that Indigenous sexualities can resurge. They resist heteronormative colonialism; they embody the possibility of radical resurgence. Indigenous sexualities matter beyond sexual politics because they expand the political imagination, not sexual vocabularies. It is not the decolonisation of Indigenous lifeways alone that is at stake. It is the diversification of ways of knowing that is at stake, our ability to emancipate from one single system of codifying sexualities.

To Indigenise sexualities is a theoretical project: in the sense of moving beyond categorisations and political borders, in the sense of making visible how colonialism and sexuality interact within the perverse logic of modernity. Scholars have exposed the heteronormativity of colonialism (Smith 2010), and insisted on the value of decolonising queer studies and queer decolonial studies (Driskill et al. 2011; Rifkin 2011). In this chapter, we showed how language evokes – and resists – political dynamics. We value Indigenous languages for the plurality of gender roles and sexual practices they encompass. But they do much more than simply expand sexual repertoires. As Fernandes and Arisi (2017) rightly claim, Indigenous sexualities matter because of what we can learn from them, not about them. Indigenous sexualities expand the imagination with new epistemologies.

References

Aspin, Clive, and Jessica Hutchings. 2007. "Reclaiming the past to inform the future: Contemporary views of Maori sexuality." *Culture, Health & Sexuality* 9 (4): 415–427.

Baird, Ian G. 2015. "Translocal assemblages and the circulation of the concept of 'indigenous peoples' in Laos." *Political Geography* 46: 54–64.

Blackwood, Evelyn. 1984. "Sexuality and gender in certain Native American tribes: The case of cross-gender females." *Signs* 10 (1): 27–42.

Cabeza de Vaca, Alvar Nuñez. 1993. *Castaways: The Narrative of Alvar Nuñez Cabeza de Vaca*. Berkeley, CA: University of California Press.

Carvajal, Federico. 2003. *Butterflies will burn: Prosecuting Sodomites in Early Modern Spain and Mexico*. Austin, TX: University of Texas Press.

Driskill, Qwo-Li, ed. 2011. *Queer Indigenous studies: Critical interventions in theory, politics, and literature*. Tucson, AZ: University of Arizona Press.

Fernandes, Estevão Rafael, and Barbara M. Arisi. 2017. *Gay Indians in Brazil*. Berlin, Germany: Springer.

Hindess, Barry. 2007. "The past is another culture." *International Political Sociology* 1 (4): 325–338.

Horswell, Michael J. 2005. *Decolonizing the Sodomite: Queer Tropes of Sexuality in Colonial Andean Culture*. Austin, TX: University of Texas Press.

Katz, Jonathan N. 2007. *The Invention of Heterosexuality*. Chicago, IL: Chicago University Press.

Kauanui, Kehaulani. 2008. *Hawaiian Blood: Colonialism and the Politics of Sovereignty and Indigeneity*. Durham, NC: Duke University Press.

Mirandé, Alfredo. 2017. *Behind the Mask: Gender Hybridity in a Zapotec*

Community. Tucson, AZ: University of Arizona Press.

Morgensen, Scott Lauria. 2011. *Spaces between us: Queer settler colonialism and indigenous decolonization*. Minneapolis, MN: University of Minnesota Press.

Murray, David AB. 2003. "Who is Takatāpui? Māori language, sexuality and identity in Aotearoa/New Zealand." *Anthropologica* 45 (2): 233–244.

Olita, Ivan. 2017. "Third Gender: An Entrancing Look at México's Muxes." Artistic Short Film. National Geographic, Short Film Showcase, February 2017.

Rahman, Monmin. 2014 *Homosexualities, Muslim Cultures and Modernity*. London: Palgrave Macmillan.

Rifkin, Mark. 2011. *When did Indians become straight? Kinship, the history of sexuality, and native sovereignty*. Oxford, UK: Oxford University Press.

Robertson, Carol E. 1989. "The māhū of Hawai'i (an art essay)." *Feminist Studies* 15 (2): 313.

Roscoe, Will. 1998. *Changing Ones: Third and Fourth Genders in Native North America*. Basingstoke, UK: Palgrave.

Ruvalcaba, Héctor Domínguez. 2016. *Translating the Queer: Body Politics and Transnational Conversations*. London, UK: Zed Books.

Seth, Vanita. 2010. *Europe's Indians: Producing Racial Difference, 1500–1900*. Durham, NC: Duke University Press.

Sigal, Pete. 2011. *The flower and the scorpion: Sexuality and ritual in early Nahua Culture*. Durham, NC: Duke University Press.

Sigal, Pete. 2007. "Queer nahuatl: Sahagún's faggots and sodomites, lesbians and hermaphrodites." *Ethnohistory* 54 (1): 9–34.

Smith, Andrea. 2010. "Queer theory and native studies: The heteronormativity of settler colonialism." *GLQ: A Journal of Lesbian and Gay Studies* 16 (1–2): 41–68.

Taiaiake, Alfred and Jeff Corntassel. 2005. "Being Indigenous: Resurgences Against Contemporary Colonialism." *Government and Opposition* 40 (4): 597–614.

Te Awekotuku, Ngahuia. 1996. "Maori: People and culture." *Maori Art and Culture*: 114–46.

Te Awekotuku, Ngahuia. 2005. "He Reka Ano: same-sex lust and loving in the ancient Maori world." *Outlines Conference: Lesbian & Gay Histories of Aotearoa*, 6–9. Wellington, New Zealand: Lesbian & Gay Archives of New Zealand.

Tikuna, Josi and Manuela Picq. 2016. "Queering Amazonia: Homo-Affective Relations among Tikuna Society." *Queering Paradigms V: Queering Narratives of Modernity* edited by Marcelo Aguirre, Ana Maria Garzon, Maria Amelia Viteri and Manuela Lavinas Picq. 113–134. Bern, Switzerland: Peter Lang.

Van Deusen, Nancy. 2015. *Global Indios: The Indigenous Struggle for Justice in Sixteenth-Century Spain*. Durham, NC: Duke University Press.

Weismantel, Mary. 2004. "Moche sex pots: reproduction and temporality in ancient South America." *American Anthropologist* 106 (3): 495–505.

Wolf, Eric. 1982. *Europe and the People Without History*. Berkeley, CA: University of California Press.

5

Doing Sex Right in Nepal: Activist Language and Sexed/ Gendered Expectations

LISA CAVIGLIA

Introduction: Sexual Minorities in Nepal

As I met S. back in 2009, he introduced himself as a confident 'transgender' (using the English term) committed to the cause of minorities in Nepal. Yet this identity was not promoted at all times in his everyday interactions – much dependent on the consequences such disclosure would have. For the sake of his family, he embodied the role of a male householder, accepting to marry a woman that his family would approve of. S.'s adjustments, however, were also enacted vis-à-vis the gender non-conforming community. I realised this as I was invited to a ceremony in his natal village a few kilometres outside of Kathmandu city. I was not the only guest from abroad participating in the event: a foreign volunteer, working in support of gender non-conforming activism in Nepal, had also been asked to join the celebrations. Differently from the latter, however, I knew what the festivities were for: the formalisation of the marital union between S. and a woman deemed of appropriate caste and social standing by his immediate family. S. masked this convivial event as his own birthday party in front of the other foreign guest, introducing his wife as his sister-in-law and cautioning me not to talk about the actual intentions of the occurrence. He feared not only the guest's potential disapproval, but also the possible passing of the word to the organisation to which he was affiliated and upon which his livelihood depended at the time. I was taken a little aback by what seemed an unusual performance of 'transgender-ness' in front of the visitor: having known S. for a while, I was exposed to an unprecedented emphasis in his behaviour. He appeared to over-perform an identity to keep up what he felt was apt and expected of a gender non-conforming person.

Specifically he emphasised through words and behaviour his belonging to a 'transgender' community, both local as well as transnational. Hence, in the same way in which he did not feel free to be 'his transgender self' within the kinship context, he appeared also curbed in front of the foreign delegate and, by extension, the gender non-conforming community, in fear they would reprehend his actions as a form of betrayal.

Nepal is one of the many sites that have been affected by a discursive 'revolution': this concerns the ways in which sexuality has been progressively addressed, as well as the identities thereby ensuing. In part, these were engendered and gained particular significance during the 1990s, as health development measures were introduced in the country. 'Target groups' were identified on the basis of sexual behaviours marked as 'other' within a heteronormative model (Kotiswaran 2011, 8; Caviglia 2018, 58): 'men who have sex with men' (MSM), transgender individuals, sex workers and more became social collectives at which preventive and curative action should be directed. These sexual nomenclatures gained global outreach and meaning, Nepal providing a particular case study of how such global dynamics play out within the interstices of local reality (Altman 2001, 86; Caviglia 2018).

Nepal's sexual landscape has seen significant progress in terms of legal and social recognition of minorities (Boyce and Coyle 2013; Coyle and Boyce 2015). The work of activists in this realm has not only improved the lives of people non-conforming to heteronormative roles, but also their political stance as Nepal's citizens. An exemplary ramification of this has been the legal recognition of *tesro lingi,* 'third gender', as a category beyond the normative binary 'male' and 'female', which encompasses a broad range of identities (Bochenek and Knight 2012, 13). In 2007 the Supreme Court 'ruled that individuals should have their gender legally recognised based on "self-feeling" and that they should not have to limit themselves to "female" or "male"' (Knight 2015). Legal measures have been set in place since then, which culminated in 2013 with the granting of legal citizenship to gender non-conforming individuals (Deutsche Welle 2015). Identity documents now mention the category "O" for "other" in passports, and *tesro lingi* in national identity cards (UNDP, Williams Institute 2014; Knight 2015; Pluciska 2015; as well as information from local informants).

Overall such developments have provided a 'language of rights' to which people with alternative genders and sexualities can associate and identify, and upon which they can unite as a group with needs, causes, and demands to fight for (Boyce and Coyle 2013). However, the everyday lives of gender non-conforming individuals in Nepal remain inserted into kinship mores and gendered practices that disadvantage them both materially and socially

(Coyle and Boyce 2015). By non-conforming to local heteronormative expectations, they are often excluded from familial wealth and education, as well as work opportunities in the free market and other sectors. Furthermore, gender non-conforming individuals in Nepal oscillate more fluidly between gendered behaviours and sexual practices than the terminology in circulation is able to encompass.

This case study reveals a paradoxical turn of events in the lives of some gender non-conforming individuals in Nepal, especially those who have been in, or are currently involved with, activist groups in the country. It is within these communities that episodes of perceived discrimination and marginalisation have been reported. These are tied to varying understandings of 'sexual identities' and identification promoted by activist movements. Those not 'complying' with certain expectations of non-conformity, perhaps because they oscillate between familial obligations and their alternative (sexual and gendered) identities, are found to juggle uncomfortably between these two spheres, perceiving exclusion and marginalisation at both ends – within their families and immediate communities, as well as the very activist milieu in which they hoped to find solace.

This article stems from broader research on commercial sex in Kathmandu, Nepal (Caviglia, 2018). The latter ethnographic investigation approaches various actors involved in sex work, understood in the broadest sense of the term: these included street workers as well as what are locally referred to as 'establishment-based' sex workers, mostly operating in so called 'dance bars' and other venues[1]. Those identified as sex workers in these sites were mainly *cis* gendered women living up to and performing heteronormative sexualised acts – though not conforming to local standards of propriety – in exchange for retribution. Overall, the work is concerned with the deconstruction of the 'sex worker' category, an approach that I refrain – to some extent – here.

In this essay, I turn to transgender sex workers who were also part of the Kathmandu scene. When I refer to gender non-conforming individuals, I am talking about the experience shared by those who do not fit *cis* gendered female or male identities. Specifically, I share the experiences of respondents

[1]   Fieldwork for this project took place over a period of approximately 10 months between 2009 and 2010 (funded by the German Research Foundation, Deutsche Forschungsgemeinschaft, within the Cluster of Excellence 270 'Asia and Europe in a Global Context' at Heidelberg University). Some of the interviews included in this article were undertaken during month-long visits in 2015 and 2016, in the context of a research project investigating labour migration in the sex entertainment and domestic sector (funded by the Gender Equality Section of the Faculty of Humanities and Social Sciences of the Humboldt Universität zu Berlin).

sexed as male at birth, but *also* desiring the performance of actions and/or appearance gendered as female by society and/or expressing sexual desires for those considered of their same birth-assigned sex.[2] The stories below point to some of the possible constrictions of the term transgender and hence I choose to use gender non-conforming throughout. The 'transgender' category remains nevertheless of importance, as I hope will become clear.

Oscillating Between Conformity and Non-Conformity

The anecdote introducing this paper illustrates the need for sexual minorities in Nepal to keep appearances and respectability, lest they run the risk of social demise. Insights on homoerotic behaviour by Tamang (2003) have revealed how 'male-to-male' sex 'may not be so much an expression of personal identity, but one of opportunity, accessibility and desire for semen discharge' (Tamang 2003, 252–253). A flipside to this observation is advanced here, in that gender conformity by individuals otherwise identifying as non-conforming should not be read as indicative of a 'lack of gender-reflective identification' but as due to 'the risks posed to their economic livelihoods' (Coyle and Boyce 2015, 24). Marriage is, for many, a way of guaranteeing access to familial wealth, from which they would otherwise be excluded. In Nepal, as in many locations elsewhere, kinship and other intimate relations are fraught by material and economic transactions (Caviglia 2018). The instance presented here may be framed as a form of 'patriarchal bargain' à la Kandiyoti (1988), whereby actors adjust to a set of gendered expectations in order to gain the greatest possible advantage within a set of constraining conditions. In addition to this material consideration, S.'s pressure to conform taps deeper within the local kinship fabric: it is tied to moralising concepts of 'honour' (*ijjat*), the blemishing of which, through the non-conformity of even one member, would compromise the reputation of entire households (McHugh, 1998; Liechty 2003; Caviglia 2018, among others). Finally S. also longed for long-term commitment and a family. Giving in to heteronormative practices was the only way in which he felt that he could tap into such a lifestyle (Caviglia 2018).

But such strategies were perceived by some of those involved, S. included, as risky in an unexpected way. A number of the gender non-conforming men I met in Nepal in fact were placed under a lot of pressure to fulfil their marital and kinship duties. Many of them were married to women in acquiescence to their families' insistence. However much to their dismay, their choices negatively impacted their membership within the gender non-conforming

---

[2]   See Knight et al. (2015) for more details on the various sexual/gendered identities in Nepal, the complexity of their expression and the multiple attachments a single individual may demonstrate with several categorical definitions.

community. An exemplary case in point was provided by some of the individuals affiliated with the Blue Diamond Society (BDS), an organisation that has been a central player in the context of sexual minorities' rights in Nepal. The organisation was created in 2001 'with the mission to improve the sexual health, human rights and well-being of sexual and gender minorities in Nepal including third-genders, gay men, bisexuals, lesbians, and other men who have sex with men'.[3]

Involvement with the organisation provided some gender non-conforming individuals with many benefits, but also struggles, which influenced some gender non-conforming individuals' professional lives and by implication their livelihoods:

> BDS thinks that if people [within the organisation] are married [intending a heteronormative marriage], the other people in the society think negative. ... [BDS] wants to promote empowerment and encouragement ... if they [BDS] know I am married, they will be angry, because they are working for human rights, and we are not following them. They will send us away from BDS because they think we are doing a bad thing by getting married, since I am working for this community (Gender non-conforming community member, Kathmandu, March 2010).

Hence, those who chose to bend the expectations of 'non-conformity' and perform heteronormative practices also seemed to bear livelihood-related consequences. The advent of NGO and activist organisations working towards the rights and protection of gender and sexual minorities in Nepal also brought professional potential for such disenfranchised communities: many in fact were offered work within these institutions as peers, mentors, and administrative staff (Fieldwork notes; see also Coyle and Boyce 2015). These were of course very welcome opportunities in a context where gender non-conforming individuals often reported either not finding or losing work by virtue of discriminating attitudes (Oli and Onta 2012; Singh et al. 2012; Wilson et al. 2011; Coyle and Boyce 2015). At the time of BDS's establishment, some of my informants reported they were encouraged to 'come out' by the organisation members and offered attractive work. But for some this security appeared to crumble in the face of what was perceived as gender conforming behaviour, expressed through their participation in heteronormative marital arrangements:

---

[3]   http://www.bds.org.np/about-us/

> They (NGO staff members) told me that I do not belong to the
> community and I should therefore leave the office/NGO ... but
> where should I go? If you had not asked me to come here, I
> would have been happy to work in my previous job. Since I've
> joined (the NGO), I have been exposed and my reputation is
> ruined. Everyone now knows me as "lady boy" in my
> neighbourhood. So in this situation, where can I go? ... Where
> could I go and work now?, I told them (Gender non-conforming
> community member, Kathmandu, September 2015).

On paper however the organisation appears to acknowledge the pressures of
'compulsory heterosexuality' these individuals are placed under, reflecting
their attempts to attune international standards to local realities (BDS 2003,
13; Tamang 2003, 229).

Not all married gender non-conforming individuals, whether identifying as
'transgender' or as other 'local' gender identities, as further outlined below,
shared the experiences mentioned above. Many had been married long
before BDS came into existence and reported no form of discrimination
against them because of this. Furthermore, timing may have played a
possible role: at a historical moment – as mentioned – when legal reforms
were being advanced, drafted, and fought for, it may have been perceived as
more paramount to stick to clear definitions and expected behaviours.
Ambiguity and fluidity may have been seen as counterproductive during these
very delicate times. This however can only remain at the level of conjecture.

There also appears to be an issue of conflation, whereby *tesro lingi* (third
gender) becomes synonymous with 'transgender' (UNDP, Williams Institute
2014, 8). The latter appears to be understood according to the definition given
in Pant (2005) as 'individuals whose gender expression and/or gender identity
differ from conventional expectations based on the physical sex they were
born into' (Pant 2005, 7; Bochenek and Knight 2012, 20). BDS itself (2014),
quoting Kapur (2012), acknowledges how 'the third space may become the
space for fomenting a queer politics that does not become just another letter
at the end of the LGBT acronym' (Kapur 2012, 58; UNDP, Williams Institute
2014, 7). Yet, accounts concerning tensions within the community, as outlined
above, point to how BDS – or at·least some of its members – may *de facto*
appear to ignore the fact that in Nepal 'sexual and gender minorities ... do not
necessarily present as such in all settings' (UNDP, Williams Institute 2014, 7).

In such a climate, the 'language of rights' that allowed communities to rise
against discrimination may have assumed a paradoxical effect, whereby
expectations concerning the 'right' behaviour and life to have as gender non-

conforming, generated friction within the community. Gender non-conforming individuals found to conform to the local heteronormative model experienced discrimination within the very community that had previously welcomed them, falling between the 'cracks' of categorical definitions. These individuals manage uneasily a life between two worlds. They do so in the attempt to ameliorate life conditions as well as gain acceptance. In the process however they feel stranded in a limbo where they lack full membership to either community.

A Language for Activism and Self-Definition

Boyce and Coyle have referred to advocacy work in Nepal in the context of sexual determination as a 'networked process' in that it was 'informed by international flows of ideas concerning sexual and gender minority rights' and the language related to it (2013, 15–16). A short documentary about the life of BDS's founder and leader, Sunil Babu Pant, reveals the genesis of his awareness of his 'identity' as an expression of the above-mentioned dynamics:

> When I went to Japan ... homosexuals were accepted there. But when I arrived to Nepal, nobody talked about homosexuals here. ... I was able to meet many homosexuals and third genders ... I began to *tell* them about sexuality and gender.[4]

During a talk in Spring 2010, Sunil Babu Pant cited the many challenges and dangers affecting gender non-conforming individuals in the country. The identities engendered by the processes discussed above allowed activist movements to coalesce, whilst providing a 'language of rights' through which marginalised communities could find support and protection, as well as legitimate expression.

> Before BDS our life was terrible, after BDS our life is good because we know our sexuality and our rights. Before BDS we did not know so we felt sad (Gender non-conforming individual, Kathmandu, March 2010).

These individuals found strength, a sense of self, and justice within the identity politics framed by the international language in which they have been placed. The potential to enjoy the same citizenship rights as everyone else turned such sexual and gender identities into tools to be used for the

---

[4]   Quotes reported from the documentary "Journey of Decade" (http://www.youtube.com/watch?v=8jq3HZ4Dr4Y).

achievement of better lives. The denominations formulated in this context also provided a sort of cleansing terminology vis-à-vis local – and at times perceived as derogatory – terms, often used as a way to insult and ostracise those non-conforming to the perceived norm. The same informant mentioned above recounts the embarrassment of being referred to by his neighbours and immediate community as *hijra*. According to Pant (2005, 7; Bochenek and Knight 2012, 20), *hijras* 'are the most visible gender minority in South Asia'. While many 'are born biologically male and wish to be female' and subsequently 'undergo castration', some 'are born inter-sexed' (Pant 2005, 7). They often accompany religious festivities viewed as auspicious figures in what, paradoxically, consists in very heteronormative occurrences: marriage and birth of a son (Lal 1999). As noted by Boyce and Coyle, *hijras* are generally perceived in Nepal as an 'Indian phenomenon' (2013, 20), with many of those being found within Nepal's confines located in the Terai, the southern plains bordering India (Pant 2005). Due to the tense relations between the two countries, the term can debatably be considered another of the perceived 'polluting' influences derived from the powerful southern neighbour (Shresthova 2010).

S. often discussed the term 'transgender' as being a more suitable denomination, tuned into transnational networks of power that granted some degree of legitimacy within an otherwise hostile context. Yet he also hailed the Nepali *tesro linghi* or *meti*, discussed further below, while also expressing through practice various behaviours and identities that cannot be easily sorted into one sole category – even more so if somewhat ascribed from elsewhere. These inconsistencies are apparent, in that they reveal how the application of discrete identities does not play out smoothly in everyday life. Fluidity rather than division provides a more accurate vision of Nepal's reality. The local *tesro lingi*, understood as Kapur's 'third space' (2012, 58), may indeed express such pliability in the performance of gender and sexuality in Nepal.

Between the Lines of Language, Everyday Lives and Classifications

Efforts to prevent 'the pitfalls of cultural essentialism' were present throughout sexual minority activist attempts in Nepal, whereby the terminology employed resulted from an interpellation of interested local community members, health professionals, and advocates (Boyce and Coyle 2013, 16). Despite this, a certain degree of reification could not be avoided, resulting in instances of discord between terminology and related expectations of 'the ways sexualities are lived, felt, discussed, or ... not discussed' in the Himalayan state (Boyce and Coyle 2013, 16).

The case study I present here builds upon this critique, unveiling friction within the activist community. Much as noted by Knight and colleagues, the individuals I refer to reveal how 'Nepal's contemporary third gender category is heterogeneous' (Knight et al. 2015, 103). Their study looks at the deliberations among activists and community members as they worked to decide who to include under such a denomination, a discussion that remains still open today. The cases and utterances presented in the previous sections are exemplary in this respect. While some of the informants stood for a multiplicity of identities, whereby individuals oscillated between gendered roles and sexual preferences, others attempted to pose clear boundaries upon the 'third gender' category. Specifically a certain 'presentation and appearance' relative to the international denomination 'transgender' was preferred when assigning membership to the group, and those not living up to expectations appear to have been excluded.

In the Nepalese case presented here, favouring English terms in the context of sexual discussion seemed to 'serve a social function' (Pigg 2001, 531): it cleared informants of the stigma that 'dirty' local terms were perceived to have cast upon them. Referred to as 'code switching' by Pigg (2001, 532; Caviglia 2018, 138), the use of English allows one to 'defuse the emotional charge of certain words in one's mother tongue' (2001, 512). In doing so, deliberations are 'sanitis[ed]' while concomitantly allowing for broader possibilities for exchange (Pigg 2001, 516). Yet while these adjustments indeed have positive turnouts for those hailing them, they also seem to limit. For the gender non-conforming, for instance, conflating the local *tesro lingi*, third gender, with the narrower global 'transgender', has repercussions for how people are 'allowed' to live out this identity, as the cases discussed above reveal.

Local terms, such as *meti,* appear to be more broadly encompassing, allowing for more fluid movement between various gendered and sexual practices. Finding origin in the Eastern Himalayan regions of India, *meti* has been postulated to arise 'from the phrase "to quench one's thirst", with the connotation that the role of the *meti* is to satiate men's (sexual) desires' (Tamang 2003, 240; Knight et al. 2015, 104). While *metis* is the term most commonly used 'in Nepal's hills areas', other terms, such as '*singarus*' and '*kothis*' are used 'in the western hills' and 'in the Terai areas' respectively (Pant 2005, 7; Bochenek and Knight 2012, 20). According to Pant (2005, 7) *metis* 'feminise their behaviours' in order 'to attract "manly" male sexual partners and/or as part of their own gender construction, and usually in specific situations and contexts'. While some may cross-dress, such practice is not typical for all.

Furthermore, much like some of the cases discussed above, *meti* identity, for those who ascribe to it, is not lived out by all at all times. This is often due to fear of discrimination, a need to respond to kinship pressures but also to assure and tap into their sole possibility of gaining familial affection and hereditary rights (Pant 2005 and field note observations). *Metis* are often opposed to *Tas*, who are defined as 'homosexual men and women' that 'act no differently to heterosexual people except as regards their sex lives' (Pant 2005, 7). While they perceive themselves as, and act as, heterosexual individuals, they take *metis* as their sexual partners. Fluidity is very much in practice in Nepal but some of today's linguistic and other arrangements appear to encourage constriction.

All in all, questioning membership by virtue of a lack of suitable 'non-conforming' practices and heteronormative roles, led some among the gender minorities in Nepal to perceive other forms of stigmatisation, such as the loss of the 'right' to identity as well as, at times, of the material means of subsistence. It is at this juncture that we could see the cases presented here as an instance answering Pigg's question: 'What comes to count as a translation of a concept, and at what points does translation fail?' (2001, 482). This could be one of those times, in that certain renditions may lead to forms of exclusion, by drawing strict boundaries around identities that are otherwise more fluidly practised. Associating *tesro lingi* with 'transgender' may lead to a reduction of 'social spaces that might allow for the expression of same-sex desire while performing heteronormative gender roles ... in Nepal' (Coyle and Boyce 2015, 15). This may not only be due to the 'growing awareness surrounding different sexual and gender subjectivities' (Coyle and Boyce 2015, 15), introduced by advocacy work tuned into 'transnational networks' and a global 'language of rights'. Rather, it is also by virtue of the expectations of advocates that those identifying and using such language to define themselves conform to the 'non-conformity' that they associate with. Those assuming a role within both worlds, on the other hand, appear to experience a double form of ostracism in which they are coerced to oscillate between and live awkwardly within one side and the other.

Conclusion

The cases and observations presented throughout this article highlight how gender-variant understandings of self are not always reducible to culturally explicit and socially evident claims to identities, or fixed across entire lifespans (Boyce and Pant 2001; Boyce and Coyle 2013; Coyle and Boyce 2015, 10). Categorical distinctions not only exclude the possibility of moving fluidly between gendered identities and/or related sexual behaviours and social rites and practices, but also impact materially the lives of those who do not conform to the expectations and compulsory non-conformity thus reified. Subsuming local terms to transnational nominal categories may not only be a process of cultural homogenisation. It may also be intertwined with how funding is allocated in the context of global sexual minority rights. As the case studies here discussed reveal, such 'misunderstandings' therefore affect individuals socially but also materially.

References

Altman, Dennis. 2001. *Global Sex*. Chicago, IL: Chicago University Press.

Blue Diamond Society. 2003. "The First Nepal National Consultation Meeting for Male Reproductive and Sexual Health: Promoting sexual health amongst MSM in Nepal." A Report. 1 February.

Bochenek, Michael and Kyle Knight. 2012. "Establishing a Third Gender Category in Nepal: Process and Prognosis." *Emory International Law Review* 26(1): 11–41.

Boyce, Paul and Daniel Coyle. 2013. "Development, Discourse and Law: Transgender and Same- sex Sexualities in Nepal." Evidence Report 13. Brighton, UK: IDS. http://www.ids.ac.uk/publication/development-discourse-and-law-transgender-and-same-sex-sexualities-in-nepal.

Caviglia, Lisa. 2018. *Sex Work in Nepal: The Making and Unmaking of a Category*. Abingdon, UK: Routledge.

Coyle, Daniel and Paul Boyce. 2015. "Same-sex Sexualities, Gender Variance, Economy and Livelihood in Nepal: Exclusions, Subjectivity and Development." Evidence Report 109. Brighton, UK: IDS. http://www.ids.ac.uk/publication/same-sex-sexualities-gender-variance-economy-and-livelihood-in-nepal-exclusions-subjectivity-and-development.

Deutsche Welle. 2015. "Nepal Introduces Transgender Passport." https://www.dw.com/en/nepal-introduces-transgender-passport/a-18638698.

Lal, Vinay. 1999. "Not This, Not That: The Hijras of India and the Cultural Politics of Sexuality." *Social Text* 61: 119–140.

Oli, Natalia and Sharad Raj Onta. 2012. "Self-perception of Stigma and Discrimination among Men Having Sex with Men." *Journal of Nepal Health*

Research Council 10 (22): 197–200.

Kandiyoti, Deniz. 2002. "Bargaining with Patriarchy." *The Socialist Feminist Project: A Contemporary Reader in Theory and Politics* edited by Nancy Holmstrom, 137–151. New York, NY: Monthly Review Press.

Kapur, Ratna. 2012. "Multitasking Queer: Reflections on the Possibilities of Homosexual Dissidence in Law." *Jindal Global Law Review: Law Culture, and Queer Politics in Neoliberal Times*, 4(1): 36–27.

Knight, Kyle. 2015. "Nepal's Transgender Passport Progress." Human Rights Watch, 10 August, Dispatches. https://www.hrw.org/news/2015/08/10/dispatches-nepals-transgender-passport-progress.

Knight, Kyle, Andrew Flores, and Sheila Nezhad. 2015. "Surveying Nepal's Third Gender: Development, Implementation, and Analysis." *Transgender Studies Quarterly* 2 (1): 101–122.

Kotiswaran, Prabha. 2011. *Dangerous Sex, Invisible Labour: Sex Work and the Law in India.* Princeton, NJ: Princeton University Press.

Liechty, Mark. 2003. *Suitably Modern: Making Middle Class Culture in a New Consumer Society*. Princeton, NJ: Princeton University Press.

McHugh, Ernestine. 1998. "Situating persons: honour and identity in Nepal." *Selves in Time and Place: Identities, Experience and History in Nepal* edited by Debra Skinner, Alfred Pach and Dorothy Holland, 155–174. Lanham, MD: Rowman & Littlefield Publishers.

Pigg, Stacy L. 2001. "Languages of Sex and AIDS in Nepal: Notes on the Social Production of Commensurability." *Cultural Anthropology* 16 (4): 482–541.

Pigg, Stacy L. 2005. "Globalizing the Facts of Life." *Sex in Development: Science, Sexuality and Morality in Global Perspective* edited by Vincanne Adams and Stacey Leigh Pigg. Durham, NC: Duke University Press.

Shresthova, Sangita. 2010. "Under India's big umbrella? Bollywood dance in Nepal." *South Asian Popular Culture* 8 (3): 309–323.

Singh, Sonal, Sunil Babu Pant, Suben Dhakal, Subash Pokhrel and Luke

Mullany. 2012. "Human Rights Violations among Sexual and Gender Minorities in Kathmandu, Nepal: a Qualitative Investigation." *BMC International Health and Human Rights* 12 (1): 7–18.

Tamang, Seira. 2003. "Patriarchy and the production of homo-erotic behaviour in Nepal." *Studies in Nepali History and Society* 8 (2): 225–258.

UNDP and Williams Institute. 2014. "Surveying Nepal's Sexual and Gender Minorities: An Inclusive Approach." Bangkok, Thailand: UNDP.

Wilson, Erin, Sunil Babu Pant, Megan Comfort and Maria Ekstrand. 2011. "Stigma and HIV risk among *Metis* in Nepal." *Culture, Health & Sexuality* 13 (3): 253–66.

Young, Holly. 2016. "Trans rights: Meet the face of Nepal's progressive 'third gender' movement." The Guardian. 12 February 2016. https://www. theguardian.com/global-development-professionals-network/2016/feb/12/ trans-rights-meet-the-face-of-nepals-progressive-third-gender-movement.

6

Asexuality, the Internet, and the Changing Lexicon of Sexuality

JO TEUT

Introduction

According to the Asexual Visibility and Education Network (AVEN), the largest online community and online archive on asexuality, 'an asexual person is a person who does not experience sexual attraction'. The most inclusive definition of an asexual individual is a person who self-identifies as an asexual individual, a person who does not experience sexual attraction, not merely the lack of attraction itself (Carrigan 2011, 2012 and Chasin 2011). However, this non-experience of sexual attraction is experienced in many different ways, such as experiencing only romantic or platonic attraction, or both. AVEN defines the community's mission is to create awareness about asexual identity. To do this, people who self-identify as asexual continue to develop language to describe the diverse modes of not experiencing sexual attraction. Both scholarly research and activism have led to emerging forms of explaining how people experience sensual, romantic, and sexual desires and attractions, such as Carrigan (2011) and Mardell (2016), explored later. These new formulations have had direct implications in several disciplines, especially psychology and queer studies. Within psychology, researchers and practitioners are at odds with the asexual community, using them to attempt to discover cures for asexuality under the guise of hyposexual (lack of sexual) desire disorder. The asexual community, in turn, resists this manipulation by engaging in research projects themselves and by developing community activism to better inform practitioners and combat harmful practices. The self-definition has permitted the community to gain validation as a sexual identity and has enabled community building to resist imposed definitions and to further educate those outside of the asexual community on best practices and available resources. On the other hand, the development of new language around asexuality is pushing queer theorists to re-examine their own assumptions, how they theorise desire and attraction, and what it means to be queer.

The struggle for recognition as a sexuality, especially within academic discourse, has material consequences. In addition to educating people who might potentially identify as asexual, information around asexuality could reach professionals who are likely to interact with asexual people, such as mental and physical health practitioners. The information about asexuality based on lived experiences must be taken seriously, and asexual individuals who participate in and create academic research need to be treated as experts of their own identities. In 2016, I presented on asexual diversity at the HumanitiesNow Conference at the University of Cincinnati. Someone in the audience asked me what is the point of creating language on asexuality and why people cannot just be instead of having to label themselves and put themselves in boxes. I am very invested in the society I am living in because I experience the material results of it, as do other asexual community members. We are told that we do not exist, that we are broken and should be fixed, that there's a pill for that, that we need some serious psychological help. We are told that our relationships are invalid, immature, and not allowed to receive legal recognition. We are subjected to corrective rape and interpersonal violence. We commit suicide. For these reasons, it is important to have the language to articulate our experiences and find communities of support.

This chapter examines how scholarship has defined asexuality and how the usage of the internet aided the asexual community in resisting these definitions imposed upon them – as well as their material consequences. I survey the depth of language the asexual community has created for itself, including its collaboration with researchers, exploring the new ways of delineating attractions and desires. To conclude, I broaden the discussion to the potential of language around asexuality for informing queer theory.

Defining and Curing Asexuality

A variety of definitions of asexuality exists within academia. In *Understanding Asexuality,* one of the first and few books written on asexuality, Anthony Bogaert (2012b) explores the 'true asexual', that individual that has never felt sexual attraction or desire and never will. For Bogaert, this is the only way to experience asexuality, and understanding this type of asexuality, he claims, enables a better understanding of sexuality as a whole. In contrast, Mark Carrigan (2011) argues for exploring diversity within the asexual community. Recognising and understanding the commonalities and differences within asexuality 'is a necessary starting point for research that attempts to understand and/or explain asexuality and asexuals [sic]' (2011, 465). Some disagree. Lori Brotto and Morag Yule (2009) argue that allowing for diversity within asexuality may attract people to identify as asexual when they are actually not, especially in academic research studies. Eunjung Kim (2010) disputes this by looking at lived experiences. According to Kim, 'many narratives of individuals demonstrate that asexuality escapes monolithic definition, simple behaviour [sic] patterns, bodily characteristics, and identities despite some researchers' efforts to draw a clear boundary for the "condition"'. (2010, 158). Concretely, individuals who self-identify as asexual understand themselves in a variety of ways which are not monolithic, but fluid and changing, and cannot be defined in static or rigid terms – as is the case with most identities.

In the face of definitions purported on asexual people by some researchers, Kim argues that asexuality itself escapes these boundaries and asexual people perpetuate diversity through attempts at understanding themselves. For Carrigan (2011), asexual community members transform these boundaries and definitions through their collective activity. Asexual individuals can shape the conversation about their identity by resisting current narratives and forming new ones about asexual identity inside and outside academia. This requires collaboration, such as when asexual individuals research asexuality in academia or participate in research studies. Asexual people can also create knowledge that the asexual community can then incorporate into educational and awareness efforts.

The most crucial struggle around asexuality is being named a sexual desire disorder, specifically hyposexual desire disorder (HSDD), and not a legitimate sexuality. While many of these discussions are theoretical (Bogaert 2008; Brotto 2010; Brotto et al. 2015), the resulting reality for asexual individuals is not. Andrew Hinderliter (2013) states that one of the goals for the asexual community is for asexuality to be seen as a legitimate sexuality like others, not something to be cured. For an asexual individual diagnosed with HSDD (Chasin 2013), treatments can range from low dose testosterone treatments (for women) that are not approved by the FDA (Snabes and Simes 2009) to sex therapy, cognitive-behaviour therapy, flibanserin (female Viagra), oestrogen therapy, testosterone treatments, and other alternative medicines (Simon 2009). Keesha Ewers (2014) explains that many females worldwide suffer from HSDD, and several of these cases are a result of past negative experiences with sexual activity that has altered the brain's wiring. Using something called the HURT model, these women can rewire their brains to heal the trauma and continue with sexual activity. Alyson Spurgas (2015) recalls interviews with women being treated for low female desire with Mindfulness-Based Cognitive Behavioural Therapy, part of which includes sexual role playing, which some participants realised was conditioning them for female receptivity (for male penetrative acts) instead of increasing their own desire for the acts. These merely 'rational knowledge claims' (Haraway 1988) become the justification for imposing potentially harmful and irrevocable 'cures' on individuals who have nothing wrong with them.

Taking back control of the narratives and the very definition of what it means to be an asexual person is not merely educational activism but a form of anti-violence activism. In *The Beginning and End of Rape: Confronting Sexual Violence in Native America*, Sarah Deer (2015) discusses the harm that sexual violence does to identity:

> If our sexuality is part of that which defines who and what each of us is, then it is at the very core of our self-identity. I think this is because the very nature of sexuality represents the best of humanity – the creation of new life, or the sharing of deep mutual affection and attraction. When this manifestation of our humanity is violated, it has life-changing ramifications for one's feelings about self, others, justice, and trust. (xvi-xvii)

Deer's argument is for autonomy over one's own sexuality as part of one's own humanity, something that is violated with sexual violence. Likewise, the same logic can be applied to the asexual community. The denial of autonomy in defining one's own sexuality is a denial of humanity that also has 'life-changing ramifications' such as suicidal ideations, interpersonal violence, lack of trust of others and medical/psychological practitioners, and lack of education around identity, an injustice in itself, as mentioned in the introduction.

While Deer articulates that sexual violence is a weapon of war and means of control and power, I argue that systematically denying self-definition and autonomy is also violence. Both are different and distinct types of violence, but violence nonetheless. Researchers who support the pathologisation of asexuality as a sexual disorder are building an institutional response to lack of sexual attraction that treats patients on the assumption that everyone should want to engage in – heterosexual – sexual activity. This institutional response is fuelled by interpersonal interactions – the idea that, within society, people interact with each other under the assumption that everyone should want to engage in heterosexual sexual activity. These interactions push people into seeking medical interventions and personal counselling, which attempts to 'cure' asexual individuals and which, in turn, further fuels the interpersonal responses, a revolving cycle that perpetuates itself. There is nothing new about curing sexuality with an interconnected web of violence.

Chasin (2017) notes that sexuality as a category exists as a divisive political issue that separates people to discriminate, criminalise, and cure.

Creating Language to Match Experience

In 2015, I was asked to lead the asexual identity forum at the Midwest Bisexual Lesbian Gay Transgender Ally College Conference, one of the largest LGBT conferences in the US. The conference organiser had asked me to encourage naming identities in the room. I stated my romantic and sexual identity, asking participants to do the same. For the next twenty minutes, the 80 participants took turns stating their identities, explaining the terms they used, and affirming each other's identities. For many of us in the room, myself included, that was the first time we had met another asexual person face-to-face, let alone another person that identified using the same exact language we used.

While meeting other asexual people in real life is becoming less rare because of conferences and meet-up groups, the asexual community became a community because of the internet. The first widely-used asexual community is AVEN, created in 2001 as a web forum. The largest asexual community exists on tumblr, a community blogging website. Both of these websites are free, and both are based in the United States. According to the 2014 asexual census, which asked participants about their identities as well as if/how they engage with a larger asexual community, the tumblr asexual community is the most widely used platform (53.9%) with AVEN coming second (28.3%). The rest of the respondents reported using other social media like Facebook, Reddit, Livejournal, Meetup, and Twitter (14.25%) (AVEN survey team 2014). Following this trend, the 2015 asexual census reported that one third of respondents first heard of asexuality on tumblr and about a fifth on other internet websites (such as AVEN, Wikipedia, and personal blogs) (Bauer et al. 2017).

The asexual community uses the internet to meet, share experiences and advice, do activism, and conduct academic research. However, these are not fully separate spheres. Educating others about identity is a form of activism. Conducting research requires people to share their experiences. Sharing experiences has allowed us as a community to create new language to delineate a variety of attractions and desires that had previously been unnamed. What happens on the internet affects what happens in the non-virtual world. Activists have collaborated to create content that is used in an educational context, such as in Safe Zone or Asexuality 101 training at colleges. Community members have collaborated with academic researchers to publish better research on asexuality, including the *ABC's of LGBT+*

(Mardell 2016), one of the first books to include asexual identity concepts as a way of informing all sexual identities.

In their book, Mardell (2016) identifies as an activist who started as a YouTube blogger; the book was made possible with the knowledge and expertise of fellow bloggers and activists. Before addressing any of the identities in the book, Mardell first takes 20 pages to talk about how identities are experienced on spectrums, including the experience of sexual attraction (none to lots), conditions required for attraction to be felt (total stranger to intimate relationship), intensity of experiencing gender (apathetic to strongly), and intensity of experiencing attraction (none to strongly). While all of these spectrums are illustrated in a linear way, Mardell acknowledges that identity is complex and cannot be captured in neat definitions or on paper.

One of the most significant contributions asexuality has made to sexuality studies is the recognition of various types of attraction, which previously did not exist. While it was the asexual community that theorised different forms of attraction, as it is central to its very definition and thus was a logical step, the findings of such research concern everyone else. While Bogaert (2012b) makes the distinction between romantic and sexual attraction, the asexual community defines and recognises at least five different types of attraction: *sexual, sensual, romantic, platonic*, and *aesthetic. Sexual attraction* refers to the desire for genital contact or sex, however that sex may occur, whereas *sensual attraction* denotes the desire for physical, non-genital, contact with the person. *Romantic attraction* is characterised by the desire for a romantic relationship with a person. This relationship may include elements of physical and/or genital contact between the persons involved, but that contact is not necessary for the relationship. *Platonic attraction* indicates the desire for a relationship between persons with no element of the romantic, sensual, or sexual relationship or any physical intimacy. A platonic relationship, however, may be as intimate as any of these three because intimacy within a relationship is not defined by physical contact. Finally, *aesthetic attraction* is defined by receiving pleasure or satisfaction from the appearance of a person, in a non-sexual manner. With aesthetic attraction, the attraction is not based on a desire to form some sort of relationship with a person. It is like saying, 'I like the way you look, but not in a sexual or even romantic way'. These five types of attraction can be overlapping or interchangeable in certain circumstances, as the choice of a category is at times subjective. For example, kissing can be considered a purely sexual or sensual act, or a purely romantic act, or partially both, depending on the person and context.

Another example of the asexual community collaborating with academic researchers is evidenced by Carrigan's (2012) article on the asexual identity formation. In their research with asexual participants, Carrigan found that negotiating relationships with zedsexuals, people who do experience sexual attraction, asexual individuals have developed a spectrum of positions regarding willingness to engage in sexual activities. These positions specifically involve genital contact but in some cases also involve other activities such as kissing. Labels on this spectrum are sex-*positive*, *-neutral*, *-negative*, and *–adverse*. Carrigan found these labels to have specific meanings although they might not be commonly discussed within the community. Mixed relationships between asexual and zedsexuals can be difficult, but this spectrum, as well as other ways to categorise the sexual identity, will hopefully enable productive conversations.

Within the willingness spectrum, *adverse* refers to the complete unwillingness of a person to engage in any sexual activity because genital contact makes them feel anything from physical discomfort to extreme disgust. *Negative* designates the asexual individual that is unwilling to engage in sexual activity but does not have the visceral reaction to sexual activity that sex-adverse individuals have. *Positive* refers to the group of asexual individuals that may not necessarily desire to have sexual activity with other people but do not mind it either. Often, these asexual individuals are most criticised for 'giving in' to their partner's sexual desires because of their willingness to have sexual activity with their partner for various reasons. This sex-positive label is different from other definitions of sex-positive that have historical ties to radical feminism. *Neutral*, the fourth category, is to some extent a catch-all label for asexual individuals who do not feel strongly one way or the other about partnered sexual activity. This being just one example, there are a plethora of other words that have been created to further qualify different modes of attraction and desire. For instance, Mardell (2016) delineates many of these in their book.

Above all else, an asexual person is a person who *self-identifies* as an asexual individual, a person who does not experience sexual attraction (Carrigan 2011, 2012 and Chasin 2011). That focus on self-definition is at its core anti-violence work; it resists the notion that we can define other people for them or that we can create a survey tool to define people. Ultimately, it allows people to choose whatever language accommodates them best, even if it is no label or no word at all.

Conclusion

By examining the language the asexual community has created as well as how we use this language in forming our identities, we can understand different ways of constructing sexual categories as a whole. Returning to the question of why people feel the need to label themselves, I believe in moving toward un-naming sexual identities and, eventually, we may not have to mark ourselves or rely on sexual communities – we will have a common language around sexuality to discuss the nuances of all of our desires, attractions, and drives, or lack thereof. The categories of sexual identities and their corresponding discourses will no longer be used to discriminate, oppress, and kill. Even though José Esteban Muñoz (2009) calls us to see beyond the here and now for queer futurity and potentiality, I see the potential that the asexuality community has as queerness, a 'rejection of a here and now and an insistence on potentiality or concrete possibility for another world' (1). This other world allows us to create our own language for our experiences and identities. This other world allows us to change the narratives about our identities and find liberation.

References

AVEN: The Asexual Visibility & Education Network 2016. *Official website.* http://www.asexuality.org.

AVEN Survey Team. 2014. "The 2014 AVEN Community Census: Preliminary Findings." http://www.asexualcensus.wordpress.com.

Bauer, Caroline, Tristan Miller, Mary Ginoza, Alice Chiang, Kristin Youngblom, Ai Baba, Jessy Pinnell, Phil Penten, Max Meinhold, and Varshini Ramaraj. 2015. "2015 Asexual Census Summary Report." Retrieved from https://asexualcensus.files.wordpress.com/2017/10/2015_ace_census_summary_report.pdf.

Bogaert, Anthony F. 2008. "Asexuality: Dysfunction or Variation?" *Psychological Sexual Dysfunctions* edited by Jayson Caroll and Marta Alena, 9–13. New York: Nova Biomedical Books.

Bogaert, Anthony F. 2012a. "Asexuality and Autochorissexualism (Identity-Less Sexuality)." *Archives of Sexual Behavior* 41 (6): 1513–1514.

Bogaert, Anthony F. 2012b. *Understanding Asexuality*. Lanham, MD: Rowman & Littlefield Publishers, Inc.

Brotto, Lori A. 2010. "The DSM Diagnostic Criteria for Hyposexual Sexual Desire Disorder in Women." *Archives of Sexual Behavior* 39 (2): 221–239.

Brotto, Lori A., and Morag A. Yule. 2009. "Reply to Hinderliter." *Archives of Sexual Behavio*r 38 (5): 622–623.

Brotto, Lori A., Morag A. Yule, and Boris B. Gorzalka. 2015. "Asexuality: An Extreme Variant of Sexual Desire Disorder?" *International Society for Sexual Medicine* 12 (3): 646–660.

Carrigan, Mark. 2011. "There's More to Life Than Sex? Difference and Commonality Within the Asexual Community." *Sexualities* 14 (4): 462–478.

Carrigan, Mark. 2012. "'How Do You Know You Don't Like It If You Haven't Tried It?' Asexual Agency and the Sexual Assumption." *Sexual Minority Research in the New Millennium* edited by Todd G. Morrison, Melanie A. Morrison, Mark A. Carrigan, and Daragh T. McDermott, 3–20. New York: Nova Science Publishers.

Chasin, CJ DeLuzio. 2011. "Theoretical Issues in the Study of Asexuality." *Archives of Sexual Behavior.* 40 (4): 713–723.

Chasin, CJ DeLuzio. 2013. "Reconsidering Asexuality and Its Radical Potential." *Feminist Studies* 39 (2): 405–426.

Chasin, CJ DeLuzio. 2017. "Considering Asexuality as a Sexual Orientation and Implications for Acquired Female Sexual Arousal/Interest Disorder." *Archives of Sexual Behavior.* 46(3): 631–635.

Deer, Sarah. 2015. *The Beginning and End of Rape: Confronting Sexual Violence in Native America.* Minneapolis, MN: University of Minnesota Press.

Ewers, Keesha. 2014. "An Integrative Medicine Approach to the Treatment of HSDD: Introducing the HURT Model™." *Sexual and Relationship Therapy* 29 (1): 42–55.

Haraway, Donna. 1988. "Situated Knowledges: The Science Question in Feminism and the Privilege of Partial Perspective." *Feminist Studies* 14 (3): 575–599.

Hinderliter, Andrew. 2013. "How is Asexuality Different from Hypoactive Sexual Desire Disorder?" *Psychology and Sexuality* 4 (2): 167–178.

Kim, Eunjung. 2010. "How Much Sex is Healthy? The Pleasures of

Asexuality." *Against Health: How Health Became the New Morality*, edited by Jonathan M. Metzl and Anna Kirkland, 157–169. New York, NY: New York University Press.

Mardell, Ash. 2016. *The ABC's of LGBT+*. Miami, FL: Mango Media Inc.

Meyer, Doug. 2015. *Violence Against Queer People: Race, Class, Gender, and the Persistence of Anti-LGBT Discrimination*. New Brunswick, NJ: Rutgers University Press.

Muñoz, José Esteban. 2009. *Cruising Utopia: The Then and There of Queer Futurity*, New York, NY: New York University Press.

Simon, James A. 2009. "Opportunities for intervention in HSDD." *Supplement to the Journal of Family Practice* 58 (7): 26–30.

Snabes, Michael C., and Stephen M. Simes. 2009. "Approved Hormonal Treatments for HSDD: An Unmet Medical Need." *The Journal of Sexual Medicine* 6: 1846–1849.

Spurgas, Alyson K. 2015. "Ecstatic Therapies, Affective Treatments: Sexuality, Governance, and the Management of Low Female Desire." Presented at National Women's Studies Association 36th Annual Conference, Milwaukee, WI, November 13th.

7

Between Emancipation and Oppression: The Bodies of Kurdish Liberation

AN INTERVIEW WITH DIAKO YAZDANI CONDUCTED BY
MANUELA L. PICQ

Diako Yazdani is a Kurdish Iranian filmmaker who is now a political refugee based in Paris, France. In his documentary film *Kojin* (2019), Yazdani tackles problems of homophobia in the Kurdistan region of Iraq, both at home and among a mostly Muslim society. The film follows Kojin, a 23-year old Kurdish homosexual, to show what life feels like for members of the LGBT community in this region of Kurdistan. The film is no report on the politics of homosexuality; it provides no statistics or institutional perspective. Rather, Yazdani offers insights into the texture and emotions of daily experiences. Homosexuality becomes an opportunity to confront different viewpoints on what emancipation really means, the rights we claim for ourselves and those we are willing to recognise for others, and the burden of religion in a society in search of freedom.

Why did you choose to make a film about sexuality and homophobia when there are so many wars raging across Kurdish territories?

Is war more important than sexuality? The question itself is a problem. Who gets to decide what stories are most important to be told? Heterosexuals? Patriarchs? For the LGBT community, sexuality is not a side question, it is a matter of life or death. I grew up in the Kurdistan of Iran during the Iran-Iraq war. That war is over, but another war goes on against the LGBT community. I don't want to condemn the people of Kurdistan for today's violence: the Kurdish people have survived multiple wars with extreme violence ranging from torture to chemical genocide. This film is not to judge the survivors. Yet that is not to say that we can overlook the violence we reproduce within Kurdish societies. This film tackles sexuality, a subject that is taboo though it should be central to any politics of liberation. How do we disrupt domination, the power to subjugate and control others, whether the other is Kurdish or homosexual? I want to impose this question because I think we are beating around the bush with politics: Kurdish politicians in Iraq have reduced politics to budget and corruption, but emancipation is much deeper and relates to the body. The real challenge is emancipation of the body. Violence continues to exist within. We can either blind ourselves, or do something to stop it.

This film shows the contradictions of a society that claims political freedom to the Kurdish people but denies sexual freedoms to non-heterosexual Kurdish individuals. Why did you choose sexuality to address the contradictions embedded in struggles for emancipation?

I don't think anyone says 'I'm against freedom' – even the Salafists defend the concept of freedom. It's just that they have their own definition of freedom. What is freedom? Nobody agrees on what freedom entails.

Since the creation of the modern nation-state, Kurds have been fragmented and repressed by states, whether in Iran, Iraq, Turkey, or Syria. The modern states operate with Kurds just like they operate with LGBT people. The film shows how everyone imposes their own understanding of what is permitted onto others, over and over again. Kurdish heterosexuals are repressed by the central government of a state, and they repeat the same mechanism of repression against LGBT individuals within their own society. Any Kurdish or homosexual person can live peacefully as long as they don't claim rights as Kurdish or homosexual. The problem arises when rights are to be respected. I think that if Kurds learn to respect LGBT emancipation, then emancipation can start for everyone. But if Kurds only want to repeat the same patriarchal model of the nation-state within their own society, then they are simply reproducing violent structures of domination. There is no way out. Or, as my mother proposes in the film, we may need to create a nation-state just for LGBTQI citizens [laughter].

The sources of suffering for the Kurdish and LGBTQI societies are the same because sexism, racism, and homophobia share the same roots. We cannot defend Kurdish emancipation while denying homosexual emancipation. Are we struggling to liberate just lands? Or the bodies that inhabit these lands? There can be no real solidarity among Kurdish peoples if we remain hostages to homophobia, if we are still controlling each other's bodies.

The film depicts a Kurdish society that punishes homosexuality, yet queer struggles have gained political vitality in other regions notably with the creation of The Queer Insurrection and Liberation Army (TQILA) in the PKK, which claims to protect queer bodies from fascist Islamic forces. How should we understand these contradictory dynamics?

Kurdistan is complex and diverse, there is not one Kurdish society. Let me give some historical context. Since the 1916 Sykes-Picot Agreement denied sovereignty to the Kurdish people, our territories were split across five newly created nation-states: Turkey, Iran, Iraq, Syria, and Armenia. Today we are about 50 million Kurdish people fragmented in five regions controlled by different states. Every region has been heavily influenced by the dominant cultural politics of each state, oftentimes violently. This film tells a specific experience of Kurdistan: it takes place in the Kurdistan of Iraq, mostly in the intellectual capital of Sulaymaniyah, and engages my viewpoint as an Iranian Kurd who never joined or supported any political party.

First, the PKK is an exception, not the norm. The reality is that one cannot even defend women's rights in most of Kurdistan. Nationalism is seen as the main form of liberation. Komala, a communist political party created in 1942 in Iran's Kurdistan, started with a glimpse of a (Soviet) narrative for women's participation in the party, but it did not last. The only political party across Kurdistan that has truly focused on women's liberation for Kurdish liberation is the Kurdish Labor Party, or PKK (1978). The PKK started as armed resistance in the Qandil Mountains of central Kurdistan. All founders were men, except for Sakine Cansiz (1958–2013). She played a key role in bringing women's emancipation to the forefront of Kurdish emancipation (she was an important leader assassinated in 2013, in Paris). She influenced the PKK to create all-female combat units, and mixed units as well. When Syria's war broke in 2012, part of the PKK came down from the mountains to protect Syria's Kurdistan, the Rojava region (which means west in Kurdish), and created the TQUILA unit in 2016 to resist ISIS. The PKK also has a small civil branch in Turkey, called the People's Democratic Party (HDP). This pro-women, pro-gay Kurdish party held meetings that included representatives from both Islamic and LGBT communities. In 2015, HDP became the first political party across the Muslim world to run an electoral campaign including LGBT rights in its agenda – this had never happened before from Morocco to Indonesia. But many Islamic Kurds did not vote for HDP because of its LGBT support. All of that to say that women's and LGBT emancipation is limited to a small region of Kurdistan in Rojava (and there is a lot of work to be done even there), the most independent region of Kurdistan, and a small influence through formal politics in Turkey (Erdogan has jailed the HDP leadership).

Second, Kurds are known internationally for their progressive agendas, but the Kurdistan of Iraq carries the scar of decades of war. The long embargo had tragic consequences and recent American wars forced a brutal neoliberalism in. Iraq's Kurdistan has been the only 'free' region of Kurdistan for the last 30 years, with a local government run by local Kurds. But the local government is controlled by two Kurdish families that (corruptly) run the oil economy together with Western corporations. This oil corruption is denounced by only one political party, called Change. After the ravaging effects of war, neoliberalism rolled in transforming Iraq's Kurdistan into a big market – there are now Chanel, Dior, and Gucci stores...and even women's organisations follow neoliberal market dynamics. Iraq's Kurdistan was famous for its agriculture, but since 'liberation' there is no agriculture left. There are mosques instead, which are six times more numerous than schools and show the force of Islamic groups that are pushing towards sharia law.

Kurdish society is a Muslim society, and like the rest of the region it is prey to a trend of Islamisation since the end of the Cold War. The PKK is the only organised group resisting Islamisation in Kurdistan. The irony is that Western politicians have long considered the PKK a terrorist organisation (despite its progressive agenda with regards to gender, sexuality, and ecology) while they maintain great relations with the Kurdish politicians of Iraq (who embody violence, corruption, and intolerance). They take Kurdish oil, then look the other way when it comes to emancipation.

Many have warned about the dangers of pink-washing, notably as Israel uses sexual rights as a narrative to vilify Palestinians and justify its ongoing invasion of Palestine. How can we understand homophobia in Kurdistan without falling in the trap of portraying a backwards Islamic Tradition that is to be saved by Western secular modernity?

I do not see any difference between gays, Palestinians, Kurds, or women. Aren't racism and antisemitism and Islamophobia all the same? Oppression is oppression. Israel is raping the humanity of Palestinians and talks about LGBT rights? To overlook some forms of oppression and focus on others is a form of hypocrisy that perpetuates the power of dominants over dominated. Sometimes I see this logic operating even in progressive European contexts when people debate how much a penis entered a vagina to determine whether it was rape or when intellectuals spread Islamophobia against Muslim immigrants. They manipulate society spreading hate like Islamic leaders in the Middle East. My film is located in Kurdistan and therefore deals with the question of Islam. I know Muslims who are believers and say that their religion does not authorise homosexuality but prefer letting people live as they wish. I know other Muslims who are not believers but perpetuate hate speeches against homosexuality. Of course, Islam plays a great role in repressing homosexuality, but it would be an unhelpful oversimplification to blame it all on Islam.

Your film tackles the issue of immigration, and you are yourself exiled in Paris. Is immigration to countries in Europe or North America a route to safety for Kurdish people who are gender non-conforming?

To be a refugee is a form of handicap. The modern nation-state convinced us that a country is a body and that to be expelled from this body is violence. It is not easy to make a new body with a new land. Of course, a refugee is free once in Europe, but there is racism and Western individualism and the subtle repression of a political system that excludes non-Westerners. Every day I understand a little more the subtleties of the language of this new society, and it makes me sad to learn subtle forms of violence. It is rarely overt; it comes with words, a look. As refugees, we are already fragile because of harshness endured in the past, because of the solitude that comes with exile. I personally grew up with raw violence, and that raw violence is gone – but now it continues in lighter versions. All my life I belonged to a minority – I still do in Paris. It is exhausting. Our vulnerabilities change, but they are still there.

Exile is not a solution; it helps to survive, to stay alive. The story of Kojin is the story of many. When a Kurdish homosexual arrives in Europe full of hope for Western LGBTQ rights, despair quickly sets in because of administrative and legal obstacles. Sadness gains a thousand colours. If I were a homosexual with dark skin I would have to work in construction, my life would be much more complicated than it is being a heterosexual with light skin who works in cinema. But being a refugee is hard and I don't wish it to anyone.

What advice could you share with scholars of gender and sexuality?

Two things: first, translate your work into oppressed languages. Most knowledge is produced and circulated in hegemonic languages, whether it is English, French, or Farsi. This knowledge rarely makes it into repressed, colonised languages. It is hard for people who live in Kurdistan and barely speak Farsi to access information that circulates globally in English. How can people in Kurdistan participate in global debates on sexuality if the debates are not translated into Kurdish? Only educated people who can learn hegemonic languages can properly engage with global debates ... and as elites talk to themselves, the gap widens.

Second, facilitate scholarships for people forgotten in the peripheries of world politics. Give them ideas, not money, let them think for themselves and bring knowledge back home and choose how to adapt it to their own realities. That way they can go study and bring back ideas, adapt them to their own realities back home. By peripheries I don't mean Tehran or the oil elites of Iraq's Kurdistan – those at the centre can always find a way. I mean the people from the peripheries of international relations, like young Kurdish women who do not have the 'right' economics, do not speak the 'right' language and do not have the 'right' religion.

Figure 1: Image from 'Kojin' (2019), directed by Diako Yazdani. Used with permission.

8

Decolonising Queer Bangladesh: Neoliberalism Against LGBTQ+ Emancipation

IBTISAM AHMED

On Thursday, 18 May 2017, Bangladesh saw the arrests of men on the alleged basis of their homosexuality for the first time in its history, at least as far as is known publicly (Mahmud 2017). Although the legal instrument that criminalises homosexuality, Section 377 of the penal code, was not ultimately used in the charge sheet, the arrests marked the first time since its introduction in 1860 that it was potentially implemented by the judiciary. After decades of increasing social stigma and violence, which the state was happy to ignore (and thereby tacitly endorse), these arrests were a worrying milestone in the sanctioning of targeted persecution. Colonialism may have ended as a system of governance in the previous century and what is now Bangladesh may have become a postcolonial state since the dissolution of the British Raj in 1947, but the need for active decolonisation remains the biggest goal for the queer[1] community.

Over the course of this chapter, I highlight the clear need for decolonisation in a specifically Bangladeshi, and more broadly South Asian, context as the best way forward for legitimately and safely advancing queer rights in the country. I do so by reclaiming the histories of queerness and its suppression through

---

[1]   For clarification, queer is being used here, and throughout the remainder of the chapter, as a substitute for the LGBTQ+ acronym. The reason for this is that queer gender and sexual identities are conceptualised differently in Bangladesh both culturally and linguistically, and queer works as a better, if still imperfect, umbrella term for those identities. This is a clear marker of the distinction between Western and more local and indigenous identities. A critique of the forced globalisation of identity politics is discussed later in this chapter.

colonialism, followed by a critique of Western neoliberal models of LGBTQ+ liberation as simply being a form of neo-colonialism. Instead, I focus on the successes of the *Hijra* community in gaining recognition through reclaiming histories and the acceptance of queer activism as a part of Bengali culture as signs of the best direction to move towards. I also argue that the success of transnational movements which still respect local understandings of queerness, specifically the case of the Commonwealth Equality Network in the midst of increasing state and non-state persecution of the community, are a concrete example of why decolonisation is the way forward.

Identifying and Containing Queerness

Section 377 was introduced at a time when Bangladesh had not even been conceived as a political entity. At the time, it was part of the wider Bengal province of the British Raj, the name used for what is now India, Pakistan, and Bangladesh, as well as Sri Lanka (later known as British Ceylon) and parts of Myanmar (British Burma) under control of the British Crown. The Raj had come into being after the capitalist expansion of the British East India Company, a mercantile trading association with its own military, resulted in an armed conflict known as the Sepoy Rebellion of 1857. Following the dissolution of the company and the formal annexation of South Asia into the British Empire, it was necessary to unify a socially, culturally, religiously, and politically diverse region into one coherent jurisdiction.

Thomas Babington Macaulay, a long-term proponent of imperialism as a 'civilising mission' (Hall 2009), led the Law Commission that enacted the Indian Penal Code in 1860. Macaulay was a firm believer in the virtues of Victorian Christian morality. Part of this was a strict, Anglo-centric understanding of gender and sexuality (Baudh 2013). In the case of the latter, there was little community resistance to the outlawing of same-sex attraction as an explicit 'carnal desire' under Section 377 of the new penal code:

> *377. Unnatural offences:* Whoever voluntarily has carnal intercourse against the order of nature with any man, woman or animal shall be punished with imprisonment for life, or with imprisonment of either description for a term which may extend to ten years, and shall also be liable to fine.

> *Explanation*: Penetration is sufficient to constitute the carnal intercourse necessary to the offence described in this section.

Part of the lack of organised resistance to this new law had to do with the fact that it did not explicitly target homosexuality (itself not a named or formalised concept until the twentieth century) but rather the wider practice of what was considered uncivilised and un-English sexual behaviour. The other reason is because queerness of sexuality was not explicitly understood as a distinct identity and thus could not be defended as such (Tannahill 1989). While there were definitely regional disparities and varying levels of acceptance, there is a general consensus that intimacy was part of the private sphere. While child-bearing and traditional male-female marriages were considered the social norm, it was also not uncommon to have same-sex liaisons on the side or as the primary pre-marital relationship (Vanita 2002).

The prevalence of Bengali sources that have explicitly queer content like *Those Days*, *Indira* and the works of Shri Ramakrishna Paramahansa (all translated and collected in Vanita and Kidwai 2000), all of which show an openness to same-sex intimacy in popular settings, lend support to the fact that there was, at the very least, a social tolerance of queerness as just another part of individual identity, if not an outright acceptance of it. This openness extended to the Muslim-majority eastern half of the region (present-day Bangladesh). However, because these local conceptualisations of queerness did not stem from a specific identity or subculture, it was possible for colonial authorities to command the narrative and categorise queer sexuality from the outset as an undesirable other (Narrain and Bhan 2005, 21).

In the case of gender, Macaulay's attempt was met with structured, albeit marginalised, resistance. Non-binary identities like *Hijra* and non-Western conceptualisations of masculinity and femininity like *Kothi* existed as named communities and could, therefore, offer a stronger rebuttal to being classed as a generic 'carnal desire'. Additionally, these identities did not rely on a definition that focused solely on intercourse and, as such, could be legally argued to fall outside the remit of Section 377 as is (Baudh 2013, 291). To combat this, the 1871 Criminal Tribes Act was introduced through Parliament, which included groups like the *Hirja* and *Kothi* as being immoral and corrupt. In doing so, the colonial authorities used local narratives of gender fluidity to further their agenda of a binary understanding of gender. While it may not have been possible for the British to completely dominate the discourse around gender, they were still able to make non-binary identities officially second-class citizens, in this case aided by the strong community links that often led to these subcultures self-segregating themselves from wider society (Hossain 2017, 1419).

Both the penal code and the discriminatory legislation were aided by the wider ideological thrust of colonialism. In its push for empire-building, the British weaponised gender and sexuality norms as ways of creating spaces of belonging – and, by default, not belonging (McClintock 1995). These norms were supported by British military culture, which saw itself as being conventionally 'masculine' against the 'effeminate' Indian. Bengal, as the centre of anti-British dissent both before and during the formation of the Crown, was explicitly targeted with its approach to androgynous clothing, its lack of gendered pronouns, and its cultural acceptance of queerness being singled out as signs of inferiority.[2] The manliness of English soldiers was credited for the military victory of 1857, especially compared to the more flowing armour of the various Indian rebel forces and the losing side's acceptance of female military leaders like the Rani of Jhansi. The material superiority of advanced weaponry and the exploitation of regional divisions through bribery were conspicuously absent in this propaganda; Britain won because of its male purity and India (and Bengal) for its effete and androgynous mediocrity (Sinha 1995).

Queerness became an even more enhanced target of ridicule and policing because of a simple logistical concern. The wording of Section 377 made any type of intercourse that was strictly not penile-vaginal a criminal offence. This extended to same-sex couples having oral, anal or masturbatory sex. However, it was impossible to police such a broad definition of unacceptable desire due to its inherently private nature. Thus, queer couples, especially pairs of effeminate men, became the central targets of harassment. This is not to suggest that women in same-sex relationships or queer-gender couples were allowed to openly practice queerness. It was simply a reflection of the fact that men were allowed more freedom in the public domain and, therefore, were more likely to be seen out and about.

It is no coincidence then that, of the three instances of Section 377 being used in colonial India, the two that resulted in convictions targeted Indian men. The cases were as follows: *Queen Empress v. Khairati* in 1884 resulted in the defendant being called out for 'dressing ornamentatively' but did not result in any imprisonment as she was not caught in the act of homosexuality. *Noshirwan v. Emperor* in 1934 saw two men (Noshirwan and Ratansi) arrested for sodomy and both were judged to be 'a despicable specimen of humanity', although the charges were dropped as there was no proof of penetration. *D. P. Minawala v. Emperor* in 1935 was also against two men (D. P. Minawala and Taj Mohamed), arrested and charged for sodomy in public, spending at least four months in jail (Rangayan 2015).

This convergence of circumstance, propaganda, and feasible implementation

---

[2]   The book *Colonial Masculinity: The "Manly Englishman" and the "Effeminate Bengali" in the Late Nineteenth Century* by Mrinalini Sinha (1995) provides an insightful and detailed look at this in the context of colonial Bengal.

effectively made 377 a law that criminalised homosexuality, despite its wording never having changed. With the simultaneous explicit criminalisation of non-binary genders and evolving criminalisation of same-sex desire, the colonial period saw the entrenchment of social and political norms that effectively oppressed queerness.

The Failure of Neoliberalism

In the period between the end of the Raj in 1947 and Bangladesh's independence from Pakistan in 1971, queer liberation was not high on any group's agenda. During this period, Bangladesh was formally a part of Pakistan (known as East Pakistan). From a Bengali nationalist perspective, the two biggest struggles were linguistic and cultural autonomy, working against state-building through pan-Islamism. There are no protests on record that were explicitly about queer rights, nor were there any openly queer members of the liberation movement. It should be noted that the religious conservatism of Salafism became more pronounced in this period, taking a sharp turn away from the original Sufi roots of Islam that used to be present in Bengal. While not used to persecute the queer community at the time, this conservatism is now a substantial obstacle.

The nascent queer rights movement – which started as early as the 1960s but did not really take a more organised feel until the late 1980s – began to take shape less as a response to outright oppression and more as a way to tackle systemic injustices that prevented equality. The *Hijra* community advocated for decriminalisation mostly because it prevented equal access to security, healthcare, and job opportunities. While harassment of the community was high and there was a strong social stigma, the greatest challenge was being unable to counter these through valid state mechanisms (Khan et al. 2009a; Hossain 2017).

Hijra had already fallen outside the colonial notions of heteronormativity through which their agency and self-determination had become delegitimised (Loos 2009, 1315). That loss of native identity misrepresented the community by forcing it to translate itself into a LGBTQ+ rights framework and be co-opted into global discourses of sexual politics spreading in the late twentieth century. Instead of being understood as its own distinct gender that took elements from (while still staying separate from) the more conventional gender binary (Khan et al. 2009b, 442), *Hijra* had to rely on Eurocentric narratives of transgender activism to get any visibility in the international politics of human rights. This was a huge disservice to both parts of the queer spectrum as *Hijra* were not universally trans, and vice versa. While some *Hijra* are trans, the wider understanding of the community is one of being its own conceptualisation of a non-binary 'third gender', which also includes traditional acceptance of intersex individuals. Most *Hijra* present as conventionally feminine in their names and dress (such as how the community is often structured around a mother) but do not identify as women. Unfortunately, despite having a long historical existence and explicit spiritual roles, especially in rural areas, the constant marginalisation forced early activism to translate itself into foreign terms to fit imported categories that could be understood by international agencies, notably the World Health Organisation, fighting for HIV/AIDS healthcare (Khan et al. 2009a, 129).

Similarly, the gay male community began to organise around cosmopolitan areas and international markers of queer culture, especially after 1990. While many preferred the term MSM (men who have sex with men; making the focus on practice of sex rather than identity of sexuality), which allowed them to maintain heteroromantic relationships and marriages, the earliest form of community organising was done through the use of networking and the creation of spaces for leisure rather than overt activism. At the centre of this were attempts to create a 'gay scene' based in the urban middle class (Karim 2014, 62). Without diminishing the importance of needing safe spaces for mental and emotional wellbeing, it is telling to note that few of these early groups later took on the call for wider rights, with Roopbaan, Boys of Bangladesh, and Bandhu Welfare Society being important exceptions. As with the colonial era, queer women were left out of the equation almost entirely in these early years. Part of this was tied to the general social conservatism that made women more likely to be relegated to the domestic sphere rather than the political or activist sphere. Paradoxically, this did allow a level of security for queer cisgender women; living alone as an unmarried woman or sharing accommodation with an unmarried man would be seen as both dangerous and unsuitable, but living alongside another unmarried woman would be seen as a sensible compromise. Thus, queer women often found a loophole in social conventions to have discreet relationships, outwardly appearing as simply housemates while being able to express their sexuality. However, this safety only extended as far as their own front door, as evidenced by the persecution of women in same-sex relationships (Mortada 2013).

Thus, there were two distinct parts of the queer community that were being co-opted into neoliberal Eurocentric models of rights. *Hijra* had to identify with a wider movement out of necessity, while the early gay men's rights movement did so out of the desire for social mobility and acceptance into urban cosmopolitanism. Both cases, however, ended up solidifying conservative nationalist opposition. As Bangladesh was moving towards becoming a competitive and open market in the world economy, especially after democratisation from military rule in the 1990s, there was a distinct move by the major political parties to connect their platforms with notions of authentic local identity. While their approaches differed (the centre-left Awami League opting for a Bengali cultural connection and the right-wing Bangladesh Nationalist Party exploiting religious majoritarianism), they both rejected queer rights as being un-Bengali. Thus, by falling into patterns of global neoliberalism, the community fell into a neo-colonial trap that once again ostracised it from the status quo.

Reclaiming the Queer through Decolonisation

The past decade has seen the fight for queer rights hit the socio-political mainstream. At the forefront of every global discussion of Bangladesh and its LGBTQ+ rights situation is the 2016 murder of activists Xulhaz Mannan and Mahbub Rabbi Tonoy, the former in particular highlighted by statements from USAID, the US State Department, and the US Embassy in Bangladesh (Ta 2017). Yet, what is often missing from the simplified victimisation of the pair as targets of a global and regional surge of Islamic extremism is the context of steadily increasing rights and visibility being achieved leading up to their deaths.

In 2010, the *Hijra* community achieved a small but major victory as a government directive was passed to recognise them officially as a third gender in all forms of legal and personal documentation, an implicit repeal of the 1871 Criminal Tribes Act pertaining to their criminalisation. It was followed by directives to improve their representation as a protected class in terms of civil service jobs, the police and public healthcare frameworks. It is an ongoing struggle as ways to 'prove' being *Hijra* do not recognise self-determination but fall into outdated notions of gender essentialism that were, ironically, introduced under colonial rule. And social stigma is still rampant.

Nonetheless, this success was amplified through strong grassroots activism and community outreach, which culminated in the November 2014 *Hijra* Pride, an event that was aimed at breaking the commodification of the Pride institution and shifting its focus towards education. During the event, *Hijra* marched through the capital, Dhaka, and gave public lectures at schools, universities, and healthcare institutions. This followed the model of reclaiming queer Bengali identity in the Rainbow Rally held earlier in the same year and repeated in 2015.

Spearheaded by Tonoy, the rally was undertaken to coincide with the traditional Bengali New Year procession that takes place every year on 14 April. The procession allows for any groups to march and celebrate their role in society and culture. By having a queer contingent march, adopting international symbols like the rainbow flag but incorporating it into traditional clothing like saris and kurtas, it reinforced the history of queerness being situated within the wider history of Bangladesh. Though fraught with risks, it was ultimately successful in shifting the conversation away from fitting Bangladeshi rights into the wider global struggle and instead towards a truly local and grassroots form of emancipation.

At the same time, there was a consistent and successful push in favour of using local forms of protest and representation to further the cause. In 2014, Bangladesh saw the launch of *Roopbaan*, the country's first ever queer magazine named after the organisation run by Mannan and Tonoy. *Roopongti*, a queer poetry collection also by Roopbaan, and *Dhee*, a lesbian comic book by Boys of Bangladesh, came shortly after in 2015. Boys of Bangladesh also began using social media platforms to mobilise popular support as well as providing resources for medical care. Bandhu Welfare Society evolved into a wider queer organisation that now supports lesbians, bisexuals, trans individuals, and *Hijra*. Bangladesh's first ever LGBTQ+ community survey was undertaken around the same time, which gave a concrete demographic voice to a hitherto discreet and underground community (Rajeeb, 2018).

The violence meted out to activists was both part of a wider attack on secular freedoms undertaken by Islamic extremists and a targeted attempt to silence the community. On some levels, it did work. Many gay activists have fled the country, seeking refuge abroad – although many have avoided the old colonial root of the UK due to its oppressive LGBTQ+ asylum policies. The fight for *Hijra* rights has shrunk and is back to pushing for the full implementation of the government directives instead of the wider community outreach that had started in the early 2010s.

Yet, there the queer movement kept certain vitality. Bangladeshi groups are involved in the ongoing transnational campaign to decriminalise homosexuality in the Commonwealth. A coalition of activist groups from across the Commonwealth – where the legacy of British colonialism has outlawed homosexuality in 37 out of the 53 member states – gained official accreditation in 2017 as the Commonwealth Equality Network and lobbied heavily for decriminalisation at the Commonwealth Heads of Government Meeting in the UK in 2018. Having been fortunate enough to be in the room myself, I can attest to the group championing context-specific solutions towards decriminalisation and decolonisation, rejecting the cookie-cutter neoliberal approach.[3] The success is already palpable; a £5.6 million fund to

---

[3]   These context-specific solutions covered a wide range. Due to the anonymity and associated safety of the participants, I am not divulging individual details. Many African delegates advocated for a re-evaluation of the role of Christianity in forming social norms, and therefore wanted to improve relations with local churches and push for

advocate for LGBTQ+ rights alongside women's rights and children's rights has been created.

The Road Ahead

At the time of writing, the situation on the ground in Bangladesh remains dangerous for outright activism. Many of the men who had been arrested in 2017 remain unaccounted for. While diaspora Bangladeshis are able to engage in public displays of protest, such as the April 2018 protests in central London to commemorate the activist murders and the August 2018 celebration of South Asian Pride as part of the larger Stockholm Pride, it is impossible to mobilise directly in the country itself. Yet, it is more important than ever before to avoid becoming a part of white Western understandings of queerness and liberation.

Neoliberal approaches to rights have already proven to be flawed, such as how *Hijra* rights have been misappropriated into a narrow understanding of gender and trans struggle only, and how urban activism often leaves out those without the financial resources available to them to take part in the 'queer scene'. While these forms of activism do have the potential for community building – and, of course, for providing individuals the freedom to at least identify as more broadly queer – it is vital to avoid a neo-colonial trap. The chilling lack of success in holding the killers of activists to justice, and the complete lack of accountability for the 2017 arrests, despite international attention, are just two examples of this danger. By comparison, the successes of getting *Hijra* and the third gender recognised, and the local outreach through cultural programmes like the Rainbow Rally and *Dhee*, are a testament to the strengths of decolonisation and local empowerment.

This is neither idealism nor polemic; the trajectory of achieving rights, however small the increments, supports this. Colonialism and Western identity politics outlawed queerness in the first place and the early attempts at rights failed largely due to its association with globalisation. While international solidarity is important and Western allies can provide much-needed security, it is still vital for queer activism itself to be grounded in decolonisation. Only then can the systemic oppression of the colonial past truly be undone.

---

litigation decriminalising homosexuality and queerness. South Asian delegates preferred a secular approach of community-building that cuts across religions and undermined religious dogma. Caribbean delegates wanted to take advantage of the tourism industry, taking on the positives of globalisation by highlighting abuses against the queer community through the free market. At the same time, all delegates also highlighted local and indigenous forms of queerness that may have been left out of the conversation and which needed to be included in future discussions.

References

Bandhu Welfare Society. 2014. *Hijra Pride 2014*. Dhaka, Bangladesh: Bandhu Hubs.

Baudh, Sumit. 2013. "Decriminalisation of Consensual Same-Sex Sexual Acts in the South Asian Commonwealth: Struggles in Context," *Human Rights, Sexual Orientation and Gender Identity in the Commonwealth: Struggles for Decriminalisation and Change* edited by Corinne Lennox and Matthew Waites, 287–312. London, UK: Institute of Commonwealth Studies.

Boys of Bangladesh. 2015. *Dhee*. Dhaka, Bangladesh: Independent Press.

Hossain, Adnan. 2017. "The paradox of recognition: *hijra*, third gender and sexual rights in Bangladesh." *Culture, Health and Sexuality* 19 (12): 1418–1431.

Karim, Shuchi. 2014. "Erotic Desires and Practices in Cyberspace: 'Virtual Reality' of the Non-Heterosexual Middle Class in Bangladesh." *Gender, Technology and Development* 18 (1): 53–76.

Khan, Sharful Islam, Mohammed Iftekher Hussain, Gorkey Gourab, Shaila Parveen, Mahbubul Ismal Bhuiyan and Joya Sikder. 2009a. "Not to Stigmatize But to Humanize Sexual Lives of the Transgender (*Hijra*) in Bangladesh: Condom Chat in the AIDS Era." *Journal of LGBT Health Research* 4 (2–3): 127–141.

Khan, Sharful Islam, Mohammed Iftekher Hussain, Gorkey Gourab, Shaila Parveen, Mahbubul Ismal Bhuiyan and Joya Sikder. 2009b. "Living on the Extreme Margin: Social Exclusion of the Transgender Population (*Hijra*) in Bangladesh." *Journal of Health, Population and Nutrition* 27 (4): 441–451.

Loos, Tamara. 2009. "Transnational Histories of Sexualities in Asia." *The American Historical Review* 114 (5): 1309–1324.

Mahmud, Tarek. 2017. "28 suspected homosexuals detained from Keraniganj." *Dhaka Tribune*, 19 May 2017 edition.

McClintock, Anne. 1995. *Imperial Leather: Race, Gender and Sexuality in the Colonial Contest*. London, UK: Routledge.

Mortada, Syeda Samara. 2013. "Acceptance of Lesbian Love: Too Much to Expect?" *Alal o Dulal*. Available at https://alalodulal.org/2013/08/11/acceptance-of-lesbian-love/.

Narrain, Arvind and Gautam Bhan. 2005. *Because I Have a Voice: Queer Politics in India*. New Delhi, India: Yoda Press.

Rangayan, Shridhar. 2015. *Breaking Free*. London, UK, and New Delhi, India: Solaris Productions.

Roopbaan. 2014. *Roopbaan Magazine*. Dhaka, Bangladesh: Independent Press.

Roopbaan. 2015. *Roopongti*. Dhaka, Bangladesh: Independent Press.

Roopbaan. 2017. "Roopbaan Rainbow Rally (2014, 2015)." *Roopbaan Online Blog*. Available at https://roopbaan.org/2017/09/23/roopbaan-rainbow-rally-2014-2015/.

Shakhawat Hossain Rajeeb. 2018. "Interview." *The Queerness*. Available at https://thequeerness.com/2018/03/25/lgbtq-people-dont-exist-in-a-vacuum-tq-speaks-to-shakhawat-imam-rajeeb/.

Sinha, Mrinalini. 1995. *Colonial Masculinity: The "Manly Englishman" and the "Effeminate Bengali" in the Late Nineteenth Century*. Manchester, UK: Manchester University Press.

Ta. 2017. "One year after the murders of Xulhaz Mannan and Mabhub Rabbi Tonoy." *Amnesty International*. Available at https://www.amnesty.org/en/latest/news/2017/04/one-year-after-the-murders-of-xulhaz-mannan-and-mahbub-rabbi-tonoy/.

Tannahill, Reay. 1989. *Sex in History*. London, UK: Abacus Press.

Vanita, Ruth and Saleem Kidwai. 2000. *Readings From Literature and History: Same-Sex Love in India*. London, UK, and New York, NY: Palgrave Macmillan.

Vanita, Ruth. 2002. *Queering India: Same-Sex Love and Eroticism in Indian Culture and Society*. London, UK, and New York, NY: Routledge.

9

Donors' LGBT Support in Tajikistan: Promoting Diversity or Provoking Violence?

KAROLINA KLUCZEWSKA

I wish the Soviet times came back. I know that everyone says it, people had jobs, education and hospitals were for free. But for 'our people' [nashi] it was also a good time, because no one knew about us and no one paid attention to us. We could spend the whole day lying in a park in Dushanbe and cuddling with friends. Everything started changing in mid-1980s, with perestroika.[1] People started reading foreign newspapers, watching American movies, they discovered about our existence. – Umed[2]

Introduction

Umed misses the Soviet times. The 55-year-old man claims that it was a period of freedom for him and his friends who are homosexual. In the Soviet period, homosexuality was criminalised by law and treated by doctors as a psychiatric disorder. At the same time, the topic of what in Russian is described as 'non-standard' or 'non-traditional' sexuality (*nestandartnaya/ netradiconnaya orientaciya*) was practically nonexistent in the society, and a

---

[1] A political movement for reform in the Soviet Union, instituted by Mikhail Gorbachev in the 1980s.

[2] Interview with Umed, a 55-year-old homosexual man from Dushanbe, 29 October 2013. Apart from Umed and seven NGO outreach workers, all other interviewees identified themselves as heterosexual. Given the sensitivity of the topic in Tajikistan, all interviewees were anonymised for safety reasons. Interviews were conducted in Tajik, Russian or a mixture of these languages. All translations of quotes reported in this chapter are mine.

lack of public awareness about it offered a certain degree of freedom to LGBT people, as labelled in mainstream activism. Umed believes that nowadays, the situation is reversed. While same-sex relations were decriminalised in independent Tajikistan in 1998, it is the growing visibility that provokes a social backlash.

This chapter touches upon a problematic relationship between international norms and local practice, putting norms promoted by international donors face to face with popular beliefs in Tajikistan. Can the promotion of social inclusion and LGBT activism by donors lead to more violence? To answer this question, I focus on why and how international norms are contested in Tajikistan, by looking at popular discourse on sexuality. It is important to recognise that sexuality includes not only aspects of personal life charged with erotic meaning, but also the social construction of them –   history, practices, discourses, and identities (Andermahr et al. 1997, 245). Thus, to understand the public stance on LGBT people, I look at the local normative order concerning family and social relations more broadly, as they reflect a collective understanding of behaviours that the society considers proper. I argue that, first, donors have taken a wrong approach to promoting LGBT rights. Their approach has been based on the promotion of social activism and has drawn on the experiences of social movements in the Western world, such as the Gay Liberation Movement (1969–1974) and the LGBT rights movement (1970s onward), that have pushed for acceptance of LGBT people in society. This approach is viewed as confrontational in Tajikistan, and has led to a growing social backlash against a growing visibility of LGBT issues. Secondly, the adverse public reaction to LGBT issues in Tajikistan should not be interpreted as homophobic. Instead, this reaction is an expression of public objection to foreign interference in the local normative order and what is seen as an arrival of Western values threatening local culture and beliefs.

The chapter proceeds in the following way. First, it shortly explains the historical and legal framework of LGBT issues in contemporary Tajikistan, referring to the Soviet history of the country, and influences from and parallels with post-Soviet Russia. Second, it describes the arrival of international donors and outlines their approaches to LGBT issues. In turn, by drawing on interviews with social leaders in Tajikistan, the chapter explains common assumptions about sexuality in Tajikistan, in accordance with popular beliefs and social arrangements. Finally, the chapter draws conclusions as to why, despite the undoubtedly good intentions of the donor community, foreign projects aiming at the emancipation of LGBT persons, the promotion of tolerance and the public recognition of the civil rights of LGBT persons in Tajikistan have had a contrary effect in the country.

Historical and Legal Framework of LGBT Issues in Tajikistan

A quick look at the Soviet past of Tajikistan provides a necessary background to understand the state's and the public's current attitudes toward LGBT people. The Soviet era imposed the first form of statehood on modern Central Asia and fundamentally reshaped Central Asian societies (Mamedov and Shatalova 2016). Over a quarter of the century since independence, the Soviet social and cultural legacy, as well as Russian influence, continue to affect politics and society in Central Asian successor states (Akyildiz and Carlson 2014).

Since 1934, homosexuality was illegal in the Soviet context. Although Soviet morality did recognise sexual freedom, this freedom was limited to relations between people of different sex (De Jong 1982). Same-sex relations were seen as a mental disorder which needed to be healed through social engineering, education, and medicine (Healey 2003, 4). Homosexual discourse was absent from public life, to the extent that state statistics on homosexuality were treated as top-secret information similar to data on abortion and prostitution (Baer 2009, 1). The choice of Gorbachev as the General Secretary of the Communist Party in 1985 and the subsequent *perestroika* opened a flow of information from abroad, including art and movies, and contributed to public awareness about alternative forms of sexuality.

In 1991, the Soviet Union collapsed. Tajikistan is one of five countries that emerged as independent states in the Soviet Central Asian region. Following the dissolution of the Soviet state, the 1990s were characterised by complex processes of political and economic transformations in Central Asia (Cummings 2013). These transformations proved to be even more challenging in Tajikistan because they were accompanied by the atrocities and destruction of a civil war (1992–1997), as well as mass labour emigration after the conflict (cf. Bahovadinova 2016). Because over one million out of eight million Tajik citizens are labour migrants in Russia, the Russian influence over the country continues to be upheld even now (Kluczewska 2014).

Under Western influence, Russia decriminalised homosexuality in 1993. In 1998, three Central Asian countries (Kazakhstan, Kyrgyzstan, and Tajikistan) did the same. Since 1999, Tajikistan has been a part of the International Covenant on Civil and Political Rights of the United Nations, which does not allow discrimination on the grounds of sexual orientation and/or gender identity. Still, in recent years, multiple cases of arbitrary detention of homosexual men and lesbian women, as well as verbal and physical abuse of transgender people by Tajik authorities have been reported (Heartland Alliance and Equal Opportunities 2013). LGBT persons who manifest their sexuality in public places have also experienced sporadic acts of violence by ordinary citizens (Vechernyy Dushanbe 2011; Asia Plus 2013).

In 2013, the Russian State Duma unanimously approved the law 'for the Purpose of Protecting Children from Information Advocating for a Denial of Traditional Family Values', which bans the promotion of same-sex relations, and which became famous in English-language media as the Russian anti-gay law (cf. Wilkinson 2014). In 2014 and 2016, a similar bill was proposed in the parliament of the neighbouring Kyrgyz Republic, but was held up. Despite a high level of Russian influence, there have been no signs that the government of Tajikistan is planning to re-criminalise same-sex relations.

Tajikistan as a New Battlefield in the Fight for the Rights of LGBT people

Following the collapse of the Soviet Union, Tajikistan, like many other post-Soviet countries, drew the attention of international donors (cf. Heathershaw 2009; Kluczewska 2017). Donors, mainly American and European development agencies and international organisations, adopted a 'socialisation approach' (cf. Lewis 2012) towards the country. This approach assumes that similar to Eastern Europe, Tajikistan could, over time and with the help of Western donors as mentors, be socialised to participate in the neoliberal world order. This includes not only the adoption of democracy, free elections, and a market economy, but also the acceptance of a range of liberal norms, from women's empowerment to private entrepreneurship. As part of the 'socialisation package', international donors have been paying attention to civil liberties, which include the rights of LGBT people.

In the recent years, donors such as the United States Agency for International Development (USAID), the Department for International Development (DFID), the Organisation for Security and Cooperation in Europe (OSCE), and Global Fund, as well as the German embassy and a number of European LGBT foundations, have been launching calls for proposals for NGOs working on LGBT issues or themselves implementing projects aimed at empowering LGBT people whose everyday lives in Tajikistan are marked with stigma, discrimination, and violence.[3] Such projects included components such as legal protection, promotion of social inclusion and changing of cultural norms

---

[3]   My personal observation working in the development sector in Tajikistan 2013–2017; interviews with five outreach workers from a Tajik NGO working with LGBT persons, 31 October 2013; interviews with a leader and two outreach workers from another Tajik NGO working with LGBT persons, 19 July 2017; and an interview with a former employee of Global Fund in Tajikistan, 1 December 2016.

and attitudes among the public, and strengthening the organisational skills of local LGBT community members by teaching them marketable managerial and fundraising skills, with the aim of improving social mobilisation.[4] It is difficult to calculate the funding provided for these projects, as well as their overall impact because they have been implemented without publicity, and were, in many cases, officially framed as medical or youth projects.[5] However, I estimate that projects supporting LGBT rights in Tajikistan receive only a small part of the overall development assistance to the country. Nonetheless, donor attention led to the creation of the two first local Dushanbe-based NGOs working with LGBT people in 2011, and later to three to four NGOs operating in the region.[6] These NGOs also do not announce their target groups publically and frame their work as help to youth and other vulnerable groups.

Through providing funding to LGBT projects, donors literally created LGBT people in Tajikistan. At the level of language, LGBT people in Tajikistan, who are not related to the NGO circle and thus are not linguistically influenced by donors, do not identify with the label 'LGBT', but refer to their community as 'our people' (Russian 'nashi') (Oostvogels and Kluczewska 2014). Furthermore, the new 'LGBT' label could not grasp alternative constructions of sexuality and homosexuality in Tajikistan that differ from Western codifications of 'gay' identity and activism. For instance, in Tajikistan, it is a standard practice among homosexual men (and often a strong desire) to be married to women and have children (Oostvogels and Kluczewska 2014). In this respect, their homosexual identity refers to their second, secret life, that remains known exclusively to other 'nashi'. 'Nashi' seek the attention of heterosexual men, and do not want intercourse with other 'nashi', whom they see as brothers.

As for the impact, projects funded by donors could not achieve their aims of emancipation of LGBT people in Tajikistan and promotion of tolerance and public recognition of civil rights of LGBT people, because they draw on Western European and American experiences rather than on an understanding of the local reality in Tajikistan. Despite the fact that only in 1990 did homosexuality stop being treated as a mental disorder by the World Health Organisation, homosexual activism for the recognition of homophile feelings has been taking place in Europe since 1945. Furthermore, women's

---

[4] Idem.
[5] Idem. During my working experience, as well as while conducting my Ph.D. field research, I realised that this refers not only to LGBT-related projects, but to many projects in areas such as human rights, freedom of media, and elections, which are considered extremely politically sensitive in the local context.
[6] In autumn 2016, one of them was closed by the government in unclear circumstances.

and sexual liberation movements in Western countries in the 1960s and 1970s were accompanied by the rise of a gay liberation movement. This movement encouraged coming out, and gay pride marches became the origin of a 'gay' identity (Ayoub and Paternotte 2014, 8). Nowadays, projects aimed at empowering LGBT people in Tajikistan by supporting social movements and campaigns carry a similar blueprint. This indicates that for donors, the universality of the freedom of sexuality is strictly related to the universality of the forms of manifesting it. This approach goes, however, against the needs of LGBT people in Tajikistan who do not wish for any attention from outside, and, in terms of social mobilisation, see the solidarity network provided by their own community as sufficient (Oostvogels and Kluczewska 2014). Furthermore, an approach based on campaigning risks causing a social backlash because it goes against the local normative order concerning family and social relations more broadly, as described in the next section.

Common Assumptions about Sexuality in Tajikistan

Interviews with key leaders from different public spheres[7] indicate that history, practices, and discourses around sexuality are important in order to understand public attitudes toward LGBT people in Tajikistan. These conversations point to three inter-connected assumptions about dominant social norms concerning family and social relations that inform public opinion.

Interestingly, all interviewees were hesitant about which words to use to talk about LGBT people, and often referred to them as 'they' and 'these people' (Tajik: *onho, in odamon)*. Tajik language is missing an appropriate vocabulary, which indicates that the topic is not officially discussed. Some interviewees used the term 'non-traditional sexual orientation' (Tajik: *akhalliyathoi/ munosibathoi jinsii ghayrian'anavi*), which is a direct translation of the commonly used Russian term (Russian: *netradicionanaya seksual'naya orientaciya*).

'Right' and 'Wrong' Sexualities

Perhaps surprisingly for a foreign gaze, the distinction between what are seen as 'right' and 'wrong' sexualities in Tajikistan does not refer to heterosexual vs. homosexual relations. It refers, instead, to a broader category, which

---

[7]   Fourteen interviewees from the department of social work, sociology, and psychology at the Tajik National University (TNU); private psychologists; HIV-prevention centre under the government; Collegium of Lawyers "Siper"; cultural centre *Painter's Union*; State Centre of Clinical Psychiatry; political parties (Communist Party, Islamic Revival Party) and local newspapers (gossip newspaper *Oila*, city media outlet *Digest Press*, independent newspaper *Aziya Plus*).

concerns all kinds of social and sexual relations including marriage, dating, romantic affairs, and polygamy. 'Right' here becomes a synonym for relationships which, in the popular understanding, lead to reproduction and are sanctioned by Islam, which experienced a revival in Tajikistan after the collapse of the Soviet Union. One of the interviewees explains this point of view: 'When we want to create a family, there is only one purpose. It is to give birth to a child'.[8] In this light, according to the popular discourse, the aim of the 'right' sexuality is to guarantee the continuation of genes, and the survival of the nation. The 'right' sexuality is not necessarily exercised in a legally binding relationship. However, ideally, the 'right' sexuality is sanctioned by religion, through an act of 'nikoh' – a ritual accompanying the Muslim marriage which usually precedes civil registration.[9] A professor of psychology is explicit about this: 'The only standard sexuality is a sexual relation with *nikoh*'.[10]

As a result, the 'wrong' sexuality is viewed as the one which is not approved by religion and does not guarantee new generations. LGBT people enter into this category because they are seen as the ones who, as argued by an interviewed lawyer: 'go against nature',[11] meaning, they cannot produce offspring. According to several interviewees, the 'wrong' sexuality is not limited to LGBT people, but includes (although to a lesser degree) any non-reproductive sex, such as extra- or pre-marital sex.

What is Allowed in Private is Not Allowed in Public

Growing awareness of the existence of LGBT people in Tajikistan contributes to the perception among the broader public that their number is increasing and threatens social norms concerning reproduction. Some interviewees expressed compassion for LGBT people, while relegating them to an inferior and vulnerable space. For instance, an interviewed editor-in-chief of a local boulevard newspaper said: 'To be honest, I feel sorry about *them*. It is difficult for *them*. I think LGBT is a terrible disease'.[12] At the same time, the impression among the public that 'LGBT' is a new trend has encouraged a defensive reaction. A professor of psychology argues: 'How can we be tolerant if *their* number is increasing? (…) If we accept *this* new *tradition,*

---

[8]   Interview with a psychologist and a professor of psychology at Tajik National University, 26 December 2013.

[9]   Although the government insists on civil registration of marriage, for many years in rural areas of Tajikistan the ritual of *nikoh* was seen as sufficient.

[10] Interview with a professor of psychology at Tajik National University, 26 December 2013.

[11] Interview with a lawyer from the Collegium of Lawyers "Sipar", 22 November 2013.

[12] Interview with an editor in a local newspaper *Oila*, 13 November 2013.

slowly it will turn damaging for our society. It will have effects on next generations, the number of births will decrease. We will have a demographic and social problem'.[13] Another interviewed professor of social work reveals his dilemma: 'I should support tolerance, but the existence of *these groups* cannot be accepted. (...) Despite my background in social science and my scientific degrees, my national culture does not allow me to accept *their expansion*'.[14]

These comments point to the issue of visibility and, thus, suggest that the rejection of LGBT people is strongly related to a growing visibility of LGBT issues, which creates an impression that 'LGBT' can become a new social norm. The issue of visibility needs to be put in the local context.

First of all, there is a strong parallel between Tajikistan and contemporary Russia. Baer (2009) claims that the rejection of LGBT people in Russia needs to be seen in the context of the ideological and socio-economic decline the country has been experiencing since 1991. After decades of silence around LGBT people, 'effeminacy and emasculation, appeared as a symptom – and a metaphor – of the decline of post-Soviet Russia in general and of the post-Soviet male in particular', as put by Baer (2009, 2). Tajikistan represents a similar case, if not a more acute one. Destruction caused by the civil war and a still on-going economic decline resulted in a mass labour emigration of young men (Mahmadbekov 2012). The strong social pressure put on males to take care of extended families, and frustrations resulting from an impossibility to provide for their families, has contributed to a similar crisis of masculinity in Tajikistan.

Secondly, the issue of visibility in Tajikistan is related to a fundamental difference between the private and public spheres of life. In Western European and American societies, the distinction between public and private started to blur over time with the increase of consumerism and the transformation of the media (Habermas 1991). This tendency was aggravated by the rise of social media. In the case of sexuality, particularly since the second wave of feminism in the late-1960s under the slogan 'the personal is political' (Hanisch 1969), issues previously considered intimate, such as childcare or abortion, started to be discussed publically. Yet, in Tajikistan the distinction between private and public remains rigid. Walls of flats and fences surrounding houses remain boundaries of the private sphere, where outsiders have no right to interfere – these are spaces where people can act freely (cf.

---

[13] Interview with a private psychologist and a professor of psychology at TNU, 26 December 2013, emphasis added.
[14] Interview with a professor of social work at Tajik National University, 09 November 2013, emphasis added.

Harris 2005). In contrast, in the public sphere, there is a social pressure on people not to show emotions or affection.[15] This unwritten rule applies to all people, irrespectively of their sexuality, who are expected to behave neutrally in the public space and not to attract attention. An interviewed lawyer explains why visibility of LGBT people breaches this rule: 'Let *them* do all actions they want, but in a discrete manner. (...) *They* don't have to do it in public. I am of a *standard* orientation, but I do not announce it to everybody'.[16] In this respect, the formation of a distinct 'gay' identity and activism, supported by donors, is an extreme case of the exposure of one's sexual identity – an action which is not socially acceptable in Tajikistan.

Return to Tradition or Westernisation?

The third important theme in the popular discourse in Tajikistan concerns a conflict stemming from two trends which have taken place in Tajikistan since independence in 1991 – a return to tradition, on the one hand, and Westernisation, on the other.

The collapse of the Soviet Union facilitated religious revival and a return to tradition in Tajikistan. A member of a religious party expresses this point of view in relation to LGBT people: 'Our society is a Muslim society. By default, there is no space for *such people* in our society'.[17] In this regard, another factor which has contributed to a cementing of popular understanding that LGBT people transgress the tradition, has been the state ideology with procreation and continuity of the nation as central themes (cf. Roche 2016). Similar state-led discourses about the importance of protecting 'traditional values' and moral development of the youth can also be observed in Russia (cf. Wilkinson 2014) and other post-Soviet countries. In Tajikistan, starting from 2015, the state narrative regarding the importance of a 'healthy family' (Tajik: *oilai solim*) and children as the future of the country (see Figures 1 and 2) have been regularly displayed in public venues in the capital city. They need to be analysed in the spirit of a unifying nationalism and opposition to what are perceived as Western values: consumerism and a rise of individualism.

---

[15] In the capital city, not on rare occasions I noticed policemen make remarks to heterosexual couples showing affection in public spaces, by for example cuddling or kissing (participant observation in public venues in Dushanbe).
[16] Interview with a lawyer from the Collegium of Lawyers, 22 November 2013. My emphasis.
[17] Interview with a politician from the Islamic Revival Party of Tajikistan, 14 November 2013. My emphasis. The party was founded in 1990 and banned in 2015.

Figure 1. Quotation by the president of the country: 'All of our struggles and efforts are for the prosperous future of children. Emomali Rahmon', Rudaki avenue in Dushanbe, June 2017. Author's photograph.

Figure 2. Decorations for the 26th anniversary of independence. Posters saying 'Creating a family is a guarantee of stability' and 'Independence is our pride'. Saadi Sherozi Avenue in Dushanbe, September 2017. Author's photograph.

From the donors' point of view, in the rhetoric accompanying a transfer of liberal norms to aid-receiving countries, the latter are often portrayed as a 'backward' object of Western development interventions, 'in transition' to Western progressive modernity (Escobar 2011). In contrast, in Tajikistan, international donors promoting liberal norms are identified by the broader population and policymakers as representing 'the West' (Russian: *Zapad*) and Western values which threaten local traditions (cf. Kluczewska and Juraev, forthcoming). A complaint by one interviewee summarises this point of view: 'These [international] organisations constantly invest money here and spread their propaganda. At this point the country cannot really prevent *this* [rise of LGBT people]'.[18]

Thus, the issue here concerns a normative conflict between a foreign codification of LGBT discourse and local traditions. This rejection of what are perceived as Western values in Tajikistan refers to a broader trend of resistance, which can be observed in Muslim countries and communities, to Western 'homocolonialism' (Rahman 2014) which refers to Western exceptionalism legitimising the expansion of LGBT rights worldwide (cf. Bosia 2014). In Tajikistan, the confrontation of the two, tradition and Westernisation, leads to a strengthening of the local order in resistance of liberal norms which are imported to the country.

Conclusion: What Instead?

LGBT rights projects funded by donors in Tajikistan have been more so an outcome of Western imagination than of an understanding of local realities. Problem-solving approaches preferred by international donors followed a simple logic. Donors defined the Tajik society as homophobic and promoted social inclusion by attempting to change norms and public attitudes, and enhancing LGBT activism.

For donors, sexual freedom should be as universal as the techniques used to manifest it (i.e. social movements, campaigns, and awareness raising). Yet, as the Tajik picture has shown, the negative social attitude toward LGBT people needs to be viewed within the broader normative picture, which includes such elements as the importance given to the family, reproduction, and the continuity of generations; the unwritten rule to keep one's private life private; as well as contrasting trends in the society, with tradition on the one hand, and Westernisation on the other. Seen in this light, the rejection of LGBT people in Tajikistan does not necessarily equal a rejection of a universal freedom of sexuality, but is first and foremost a rejection of its public manifestation and the interference of outsiders. The good intentions of donors

---

[18] Interview with a member of the Painters' Union, 19 November 2013. My emphasis.

and their devotion to the promotion of diversity and social inclusion may strengthen existing social divisions and even provoke violence.

The case of Tajikistan and donors' support for LGBT people raises three practical questions. The first question is *who?* Can foreign-sponsored activism lead to real social changes, in the absence of an indigenous movement for recognition of civil rights of LGBT people? The second question is *how?* Are there universal means of promoting the social inclusion of LGBT people? Does Tajikistan need to repeat the Western experience of the fight for the rights of LGBT people based on confrontations of norms and the social mobilisation of LGBT communities – or might there be other ways? The third question is *what instead?* This question is the most difficult to answer. While it is easy to criticise the activities and approaches of the donor community, it is more difficult to offer alternatives.

At this point it is useful to come back to the opening quotation by Umed. He believes that the Soviet period when homosexuality was criminalised was a period of freedom for LGBT people, unlike today, when, despite decrimin- alisation, a growing social awareness of LGBT people places them in a position of vulnerability. This might be a suggestion for donors. To avoid causing more harm, donors should reconsider intervening in countries with complex social dynamics which they may not fully comprehend.

* *I am thankful to Robert Oostvogels for his invaluable role in designing the research and comments on an earlier draft of this chapter, to the editors of E-International Relations for their support in finalising the chapter, and to all people who agreed to participate in the research despite the high political sensitivity of the topic.*

This research was conducted with the support of the Eurasia Foundation of Central Asia-Tajikistan and finalised within the EU Horizon 2020 programme 'Around the Caspian' [grant number SEP-210161673].

References

Akyildiz, Sevket and Richard Carlson. 2014. *Social and Cultural Change in Central Asia: The Soviet Legacy*. Abingdon, UK, and New York, NY: Routledge.

Andermahr, Sonya, Terry Lovell, and Carol Wolkowitz. 1997. *A Concise Glossary of Feminist Theory*. Abingdon, UK: Hodder Education Publishers.

Asia Plus. 2013. "Kto menya osudit, chto ya – gey?". 11 September, Accessed 1 December 2016, https://www.asiaplus.tj/ru/news/i-kto-menya-osudit-chto-ya-gei-konkurs-blogerov.

Ayoub, Phillip and David Paternotte. 2014. "Introduction" *LGBT activism and the making of Europe: a rainbow Europe*, edited by Phillip Ayoub and David Paternotte, 9–29. Basingstoke, UK: Springer.

Baer, Brian James. 2009. *Other Russias: Homosexuality and the crisis of post-Soviet identity*. Basingstoke, UK: Palgrave Macmillan.

Bahovadinova, Malika. 2016. *Ideologies of Labour: The Bureaucratic Management of Migration in Post-Soviet Tajikistan*. PhD Dissertation, Indiana University-Bloomington.

Bosia, Michael. 2014. "Strange fruit: Homophobia, the state, and the politics of LGBT rights and capabilities." *Journal of Human Rights* 13 (3): 256–273.

Cummings, Sally. 2013. *Understanding Central Asia: politics and contested transformations*. Abingdon, UK: Routledge.

De Jong, Ben. 1982. "An Intolerable Kind of Moral Degeneration: Homosexuality in the Soviet Union". *The Review of Socialist Law* 8 (1): 341–357.

Escobar, Arturo. 2011. *Encountering Development: The making and unmaking of the Third World*. Princeton, NJ: Princeton University Press.

Habermas, Jürgen. 1991. *The structural transformation of the public sphere: An inquiry into a category of bourgeois society*. Cambridge, MA: MIT Press.

Hanisch, Carol. 1969. "The personal is political" *Radical feminism: A documentary reader*, 113–116.

Harris, Colette. 2005. "Desire versus Horniness: sexual relations in the collectivist society of Tajikistan" *Social Analysis* 49 (2): 78–95.

Healey, Dan. 2003. "What Can We Learn From the History of Homosexuality in Russia?" *History Compass* 1 (1): 1–6.

Heartland Alliance and Equal Opportunities. 2013. "Human Rights Violations of Lesbian, Gay, Bisexual, and Transgender (LGBT) People in Tajikistan: A Shadow Report." Submitted for Consideration at the 108th Session of the United Nations Human Rights Committee.

Heathershaw, John. 2009. *Post-conflict Tajikistan: the politics of peacebuilding and the emergence of legitimate order*. Abingdon, UK: Routledge.

Kluczewska, Karolina. 2014. "Migrants' Re-entry Bans to the Russian Federation: The Tajik Story". Security Brief No. 16. Geneva Centre for Security Policy, OSCE Academy and Norwegian Institute of International Affairs.

Kluczewska, Karolina. 2017. "Benefactor, industry or intruder? Perceptions of international organizations in Central Asia–the case of the OSCE in Tajikistan" *Central Asian Survey*, 1–20.

Kluczewska, Karolina and Shairbek Juraev. Forthcoming. "The EU and Central Asia: Nuances of an aided partnership" *Managing threats to security in wider Europe* edited by Rick Fawn. Basingstoke, UK: Palgrave Macmillan.

Lewis, David. 2012. "Who's socialising whom? Regional organisations and contested norms in Central Asia" *Europe-Asia Studies* 64 (7): 1219–1237.

Mahmadbekov, Moensho. 2012. *Migracionnye processy: Sushnost, osnovnye tendencii i ih osobennosti v sovemennom obshestve (Opyt Tadzhikistana)*. Akademiya Nauk Respubliki Tadzhikistan, Institut Filosofii, Politologii i Prava im. A.M. Bogudinova.

Mamedov, Georgy and Oksana Shatalova. 2016, *Ponyatiya o sovetskom v Centralnoy Azii*. SHTAB-Press.

Oostvogels, Robert, and Karolina Kluczewska. 2014. *Alternate sexuality in Tajikistan*. Eurasia Foundation of Central Asia – Tajikistan. Internal report.

Rahman, Momin. 2014. *Homosexualities, Muslim cultures and modernity*. Basingstoke, UK: Springer.

Roche, Sophie. 2016. "A sound family for a healthy nation: motherhood in Tajik national politics and society" *Nationalities Papers* 44 (2): 207–224.

Vechernyy Dushanbe. 2011. "Iznasilovannoe detstvo", 26 October, No. 43 (727).

Wilkinson, Cai. 2014. "Putting 'traditional values' into practice: The rise and contestation of anti-homopropaganda laws in Russia" *Journal of Human Rights* 13 (3): 363–379.

10

The Commodified Queer Sublime

SOHEIL ASEFI

My mom and I were discussing the relation of communists to the proletariat while watching skyline views of New York Harbor on a ferry tour to Staten Island. She is a long-time political activist who spent time in solitary confinement and underwent physical and mental torture in Iran's first women's political prison in the 1970s (Asefi 2016). It was her first time visiting the United States. Unlike most things in New York, the ferry is free. After a five-mile journey right by the Statue of Liberty and Ellis Island, our fellow visitors on the ferry were taking selfies as we approached Lower Manhattan. Closer to Manhattan, the movement of people and freight was steadily increasing. The certain moment of the spectacular in American culture was embodied in front of my eyes; what was lost in translation was the incommensurable distance between me and the people taking selfies. The spectacular was beyond the selfie, a fad deeply enmeshed in popular culture.

To tackle the limits of translation, the term 'spectacular' is helpful to depict the use of selfies and the very culture produced under a regime of neoliberalism as symptomatic of the power of social media to turn public spaces into private displays of commodification. Without its consumption aspect, 'spectacular' is unable to depict the 'awesomeness' of the dominant American culture in the air. This simple story of 'awesomeness' is one of the most common conditions in everyday American life and resonates with complex themes like commodification which is strongly associated with sexualisation and which charges everyday objects with desire. That was my train of thought as I tried to trace the interconnection in the spectrum of 'awesomeness' to 'greatness' and 'coolness' in a conversation with 'spectacular' on a ferry tour.

Desirable queer possibilities of 'queerness' outside the 'Western'/American/

English-speaking contexts struck my mind. Nevertheless, the ferry itself was symbolic of crossing to the other side. Whether or not 'the other side' is capable of tackling the question of belonging beyond top-down forms of transnational political agency remains an open question. Putting aside the ferry as a 'means of transportation', there is also a great potential for other layers to surpass the limits of 'transnational advocacy networks'. However, the deeper level of the ferry narrative may simply fall into the trap of queer performativity which, it would seem, has become a Euro-American political obsession.

Meanwhile, the Communist Manifesto was trying to connect the dots and the intersection between queerness, the sublime, and the creation of self, 'the bourgeoisie has through its exploitation of the world market given a cosmopolitan character to production and consumption in every country' (Marx 1996). This staged an encounter with the most widely held assumption in queer theory today: that the political value of the field lies in its antinormative commitments, along with the necessity to rethink the meaning of norms, normalisation, and the normal breaking from private property forms of relationship ('love'); in other words, it necessitates the abolition of private property within relationships of production (Cotter 2012).

Closer to Manhattan, the movement of people and freight was steadily increasing. Once again, that certain moment of the sublime spectacular in American culture was embodied in front of my eyes which reminded me of transformations in border governmentalities which have affected the mobility of 'ordinary' travellers; among the 'diverse' excited crowd of the moment of spectacular, a number of individuals were the direct and indirect consumers of 'the security and development' in need of LGBTQIA subjects as key terrains in geopolitical struggles around war and security as well as around human rights and norms diffusion. As the philosopher Edmund Burke says, when we are astonished, or shocked, our mind is completely filled with the object which caused that feeling.

The spectacular moment of value creation with aesthetic capital overshadowed rational powers of a number of people on the ferry. This is the feeling called 'the sublime' according to Burke. Yet having declared New York City an 'awesome' city in the world, Lady Gaga waved the flag of rainbow capitalism in the 'spectacular' way visible from the ferry, chanting, 'make America diverse again'; Gaga's LGBTQIA diversity intersects with normative understandings of 'normal military policies', and 'normal just wars'. This sexualised order of international relations made me think of the connection between the headlines of *The New York Times* like 'ISIS kills Gays' and 'Iran hangs Gay men', and the *BBC's* 'Meet Iran's gay mullah forced to flee the country'. Yet along the exotic subject of 'Gay Mullah', these brown bodies had also become the subjects of torture, rape, and execution in the prisons of Abu Ghraib, in Bagram, and Tehran's Evin prison, where I was kept in solitary confinement for many months for the crime of being an 'independent leftist journalist'. In that prison, thousands of jailed Iranian anti-imperialist forces were killed and buried in mass graves like Khavaran cemetery in the 1980s (Asefi 2013).

LGBTQIA identity in the West is a product of specific Euro-American histories and social formations as John D'Emilio put it in his seminal and widely influential essay linking 'gay' identity with 'free labour' under capitalism (D'Emilio 1983). When this set of values became an indispensable part of the package of liberal imperialist forces for the global South, understanding contemporary sexuality and gender politics in one of the targeted countries of Washington compels an examination of the imbrications between the idea of modernity, the production of non-normative identity-based social categories, and critiques of neoliberalism. The tyrannies of sexual and gender normativity have been widely examined in queer theory. Heteronormativity, homo-normativity, whiteness, family values, marriage, monogamy, Christmas, have all been objects of sustained critique, but what is at stake is whether what remains of queer theory is able/not able to address the complexities of the situation in a way similar to the way the plights of fallen anti-capitalist forces from US-targeted countries like the Islamic Republic in Iran have been commodified by the human rights industry. As far as those large parts of a generation of macho leftists need to be studied in this regard, the history of desire and militancy needs to be at the centre of this queer study which usually tends to reduce political agency to a vague, impotent, and merely performative framework in Western academia rather than get into the importance of class and explore the sexual dimensions of different concepts of Marxist political economy in the region beyond the fashionable imperial narrative of 'democracy versus dictatorship'.

While the dominant imperialist power chooses which bodies and sexualities need to be 'saved' and which 'homophobic' Muslims need to be 'civilised', the barbaric masculinity of a neoliberal theocracy in transition like the one in Iran makes it more difficult to talk about the necessity of going beyond the Western regime of sexuality and its primitive homo/hetero binary which is the effect of a colonial epistemology.

The place where I was 'born and raised', has always been the subject of international scrutiny since the incomplete 1979 Revolution and the rise of the theocratic regime under the well-worn slogan 'Death to America'. The US declared it a member of the 'axis of evil' in 2002, under President George W.

Bush. This doctrine, the logical continuation of Martin Indyk's policy of dual containment, has been perpetuated by subsequent US presidents Clinton, Bush, Obama and Trump with each applying different tactics. The Gay Internationalists, who work under the assumption that Muslim 'LGBTQ people', like women, need to be saved from their own oppressive traditions, have co-opted the Islamophobic logic that fuels the so-called War on Terror to try to impose mainstream LGBTQIA 'values' under the guise of 'human rights'. As a matter of fact, the dangerous discourse of 'rights' has always been exported to the periphery, whether through direct military intervention and/or crippling sanctions or through foreign direct investment and the installation of 'trickle-down economics' for the sake of 'democracy promotion' – the combination of hard and soft power according to Joseph Nye (2009).

Had she been born in a different country, mom thought, and without the education to qualify as a long-time Marxist revolutionary in Iran, she might have become an American opera singer, offering her massive talent to an 'awesome' crowd in Metropolitan Opera. But the idea, explored in detail – what, who, when, where, why, how – those questions mom had obediently followed in her life from a very young age. According to Burke, the sublime is usually something larger than you, and dangerous, like the ocean, but if something is large and not scary, like a huge field of wheat, it is not sublime. We approached Manhattan, a capitalist sublime, half a decade after the riots at Stonewall; the historic place had been completely co-opted by pink capitalism. The drag queens were now striving to portray a broader image of what 'queer' means to 'politicise' sexual practices for the LGBTQIA industry. Integrating drag/trans/queer bodies into an unchanged homonormative and gender-normative mainstream which can be the subject of a radical queer theory study has also to confront the exilic yearning, capitalism (later neoliberal), and Euro-American hegemony.

As Jasbir Puar (2007) argues, the consolidation of homonormativity travels through orientalist imaginings of 'Muslim sexuality'. What is at stake is whether the word 'queer', after queer theory, would be able to wrest sexuality from the dead end of identity politics (Penny 2013). It would be naïve to underestimate the ongoing project of neo-imperialism in the Middle East without putting it into the context of queer antinormativities which are themselves captured on behalf of governing social, cultural, political, and economic institutions. In other words, if queer refers to the community of people whose gender and/or sexuality do not fit into hegemonic norms, it is the commodification of queer culture that paves the way for liberal imperialists to impose the Western regime of sexuality under the guise of 'rights' to countries in the semi-periphery (Wallerstein 2004).

Take for instance one of the stories of the Iranian liberal reporter of *The Guardian* (Kamali Dehghan 2017) as evidence that Gay Internationalists have dominated the public sphere to shape a specific mainstream LGBTQIA agenda in one of the targets of US imperialism in the Middle East. Bahman Mohassess, a prominent exiled Iranian artist dubbed by some as the 'Persian Picasso', was a radical leftist thinker central to the development of Tehran's burgeoning counter-culture of the 1960s and 70s. Yet he has now been reduced to the category of an 'Iranian Gay Artist' next to his Western fellow artist Francis Bacon to make its Western orientalist audience motivated to read the liberal narrative of victimisation under the guise of 'rights'.

While being 'homosexual' did not have anything to do with him being reclusive and he lived his sexuality fully in a hypersexualised society, the homonormative narrative of his 'national identity' and 'sexual identity' is an indication of the global political economy at work and the significance of imperial soft power exercised though LGBTQIA liberal venues. The documentary film *Fifi Howls from Happiness*, which is named after one of his paintings, provides a unique insight into Mohassess's life in exile: it goes beyond normative understandings of gender and sexuality to intersect with normative understandings of war, democracy, human rights, and the myth of the trickle-down economy. As a matter of fact, the erasure of the history of struggle for socialism in the Middle East (historical opportunism and revisionism) contributed a great deal to the imagined geographies of 'gay-friendly' versus 'homophobe' states in the region. It was key to erase anti-imperialist agency in the 'human rights' package so democracy promoters could pave the way for the exportation of any kind of colonial product to the Middle East and North Africa. Many of these so-called democracy promotion agendas are focused on the rights discourse within the framework of heteronormative pink capitalism, and their ramifications are felt primarily in the middle and upper classes of Iranian society. The working and lower-class realities of most Iranians and the complexities of sexuality regarding wage labour, meanwhile, have little or nothing to do with the rainbow packages of 'visibility' that have been exported by hashtag movements of Gay Internationalists as journalist and human rights activists and academics on Silicon Valley's toys. As a matter of fact, the pro-West revisionist historians in the role of 'democracy' promoters like the one at the neoconservative Hoover Institution's Iran Democracy Project[1] have taken advantage of the tyranny of the Islamic Republic as a theocracy in transition in Iran and have spread profound confusion about the nature of the class struggle. The line of these 'democracy promoters'/'native informers' is based both upon transnational networks and the mainstream human rights discourse – main tools of the US State Department and various think tanks.

---

[1]   See for instance the works of Abbas Milani of the Hoover Institution at https://www.hoover.org/profiles/abbas-milani.

Indeed, the topic of LGBTQIA people in 'developing' countries like Iran has been at the centre of the development of a new market-oriented masculinity that is spreading to 'heterosexual' men and contributes to the formation of neo-imperialism in the region. The mainstream narrative in the case of Iran today reduces complex social realities to a cartoonish image – pro-Western (rights) civilised 'Moderates' and 'Reformists' versus Islamist fundamentalists ('Hardliners'/'Principlists'). Having practiced a profound amnesia regarding their own past, a large part of Iran's leftists in exile follow the dominant discourse of the Western regime of sexuality and 'rights', while sexual masochism disorder is still the most significant epidemic among them and a number of men and women within the leftist Iranian intellectual community struggling to survive under the ideological apparatuses of the Islamic Republic. Hence questions such as 'has the Left got a past? And if so, is that past best forgotten?'. Phil Cohen raised this in his recent book *Archive That, Comrade! Left Legacies and the Counter Culture of Remembrance*, a searing meditation on the politics of memory regarding an emancipatory anti-capitalist and non-hetero/homo normative project of struggle in the Middle East.

Along the same lines, the dominant narrative of 'queer' identities and the LGBTQIA industry with its politics of 'coming out' and 'visibility' has been exported to the global periphery, yet it has failed to tackle the politics of belonging beyond the mainstream paradigms of identity politics. Thus, the 'out of place' concept of exile is not able to construct a non-commodified action of questioning and challenging issues on gender, sexuality, sovereignty, imperialism, culture, borders, history, citizenship, identity, displacement, and belonging. Hence, the sublime acts as a point of rupture. If the term 'revolutionary' has morphed into the sexier term 'activist' with the commodification of activism and the NGO-isation of resistance, why would the dominant colonial language based on the homo/hetero binary of the Western regime of sexuality not become part and parcel of a broader issue of power and hegemony? The way normative and/or non-normative genders and sexualities sustain – and contest – international formations of power is the crux of the matter.

While the discussion went on, we got to the moment of the sublime: Lower Manhattan. 'Cute', I had this message pop up on my Scruff profile. 'Is cute beautiful?' I asked. The person, who branded himself 'sapiosexual' on the other side, looked at me virtually with faux innocence of the wide-eyed sort. He was not sure what it is, 'awesome! Can you explain?' He asked. I then replied, 'how is awesome inscribed or translated into cuteness?' The ocean was at the end of this 'conversation' like all everyday random messages on online dating apps, a common pre-orgasmic unrequited 'queer' issue?! Adrienne Rich's *Diving into the Wreck* was music in my ear that the relations between the sexes and self-knowledge can be won only through the act of criticism. 'Where are you from?' he asked. The politics of home and memory once again struck my mind; as a writer in exile, I have confronted this situation several times and have always mentioned the fact that I have increasingly felt myself to be more an outsider in my country of birth than in other places in the world. If the home, the nation, the marketing brand of LGBTQIA are the only potential spaces of belonging, then where is home beyond these spaces which are simultaneously tied together by media messages and the workings of the real estate market, by the commodification of the body and the reification of desire (whether in a pretentious vibe of academia or on a hook-up app), and by macro factors such as the immigration policies of the state and the impact of the global economy? Is a homogeneous understanding of diasporic subjects able to depict political agency beyond the categorical assumptions of queer theory?!

The crow in Pasolini's 'The Hawks and the Sparrows' comes to assist me with the 'where are you from?' question, 'I come from far away. My country is ideology. I live in the capital, the city of the future, on Karl Marx Street'.

The man in the red tie said something, and mom, not catching the words, nodded in confirmation. 'So, you like the ocean?' he said with disapproval, and then, forgivingly, 'Most people do'.

References

Asefi, Soheil. 2013. "Betraying Khavaran" *Counterpunch* 23. Available online at https://www.counterpunch.org/2013/08/23/betraying-khavaran/ .

Asefi, Soheil. 2016. "A portrait of Iran's incomplete revolution" *The New Arab,* 17 February 2016. https://www.alaraby.co.uk/english/comment/2016/2/17/a-portrait-of-irans-incomplete-revolution

Cotter, Jennifer. 2012. "Bio-politics, Transspecies Love and/as Class Commons-Sense." *The Red Critique* 14: Available online at http://redcritique.org/WinterSpring2012/biopoliticstransspeciesismandclasscommonssense.htm.

D'Emilio, John. 1983. "Capitalism and Gay Identity" *Powers of Desire: The Politics of Sexuality* edited by Ann Snitow, Christine Stansell and Sharon Thompson. New York, NY: Monthly Review Press.

Kamali Dehghan, Saeed. 2017. "Francis Bacon and gay Iranian artist Bahman Mohasses shown in Tehran" *The Guardian*. 10 March 2017. Available online at https://www.theguardian.com/world/2017/mar/10/stunning-collection-of-modern-art-goes-on-display-in-tehran

Marx, Karl. 1996. *The Communist Manifesto*. London, UK, and Chicago, IL: Pluto Press.

Nye, Joseph. 2009. "Get Smart: Combining Hard and Soft Power". *Foreign Affairs*. July/August 2009 issue. Available online at https://www.foreignaffairs.com/articles/2009-07-01/get-smart

Penny, James. 2013. *After Queer Theory: The Limits of Sexual Politics*. London, UK: Pluto Press.

Puar, Jasbir. 2007. *Terrorist Assemblages: Homonationalism in Queer Times*. Durham, NC: Duke University Press Books.

Wallerstein, Immanuel. 2004. *World-systems Analysis: An Introduction*. Durham, NC: Duke University Press Books.

Glossary

Abya Yala – the continent of the Americas in Kuna language. The expression can be translated as 'land in its full maturity'. The concept emerged toward the end of the 1970s in *Dulenega*, a Kuna Tule territory in Panama, when Kuna activists told reporters that they employed the term Abya Yala to refer to the American continent in its totality. Since the 1980s, Indigenous movements increasingly refer to the Abya Yala in official declarations, decolonising epistemologies, and when enacting a differentiated Indigenous locus of cultural and political expression.

Asexuality – a self-identified sexual identity characterised by a lack of sexual attraction.

Cisgender – having a current gender identity and sexual expression that is concordant with one's assigned sex at birth, i.e. nontransgender.

Heteronormativity – what makes heterosexuality seem coherent, natural and privileged. It involves the assumption that everyone is 'naturally' heterosexual, and that heterosexuality is the ideal.

Homonationalism – has been described as national homonormativity, in the framework of which domesticated homosexuals provide ammunition to nationalism.

Homocolonialism – the deployment of LGBTIQ rights and visibility to stigmatise non-Western cultures and conversely reassert the supremacy of Western nations and Western civilisation. Momin Rahman (2014) understands homocolonialism as the reassurance of Western civilisational superiority through the presence of increasingly homonormative versions of homosexuality (such as gay marriage) in contrast with their absence in non-Western multicultural communities worldwide. These characterisations rely on a monolithic version of culture, purporting a uniform, static culture that delineates East and West.

Homonormativity – refers to the mainstreaming of lesbian and gay politics and the assemblage of specific social changes in a range of countries over the last two decades that appear to have had particular social and political consequences for gay rights.

Intersex – historically known as hermaphroditism, in more recent usage refers to diverse presentations of ambiguous or atypical genitals; sometimes confused with transsexualism. The general term used for a variety of conditions in which a person is born with a reproductive or sexual anatomy that does not seem to fit in the typical definitions of female or male.

LGBT – an acronym for Lesbian, Gay, Bisexual, and Transgender. It was first coined in the late 1980s in the United States, then become a mainstream umbrella term to broadly refer to people, organisations, and movements that do not identify as heterosexual or cisgender. Variations exist in the order of the letters (e.g. GLBT) as well as in the identities listed in the acronym (e.g. LGBTQI) to reflect the sexual and gender diversity that permeate these communities.

Pinkwashing – political and corporate strategies that use support for LGBT sexualities as self-promotion and branding rather than human rights. Israel promoted an LGBTQ-friendly image by supporting Pride celebrations and same-sex rights to reframe the occupation of Palestine in terms of civilisational narratives and divert attention from human rights abuses and territorial occupation with the discourses of (sexual) modernity (Puar 2011; Stern 2017).

Pride – A generally positive stance to promote LGBTQ self-affirmation, rights, and dignity, and to oppose any discrimination and violence against those groups. Like the term 'LGBT', Pride has been used to increase the visibility of people and communities who self-identify as non-heterosexual and/or non-cisgender, initially in Anglophone countries and places. The term also refers to events that celebrate sexual diversity, most commonly in the form of a parade, to raise awareness about sexual freedoms and build social ties for LGBT people.

Queer – used to describe those with non-normative gender, either as an umbrella term or a stand-alone identity, typically encompassing those who are both male and female, neither male nor female, moving between both genders, or otherwise 'queer' in gender presentation. Originally, the term meant 'odd' or 'peculiar', and was used as a slur against non-heterosexual behaviour. It was then re-appropriated by activists and scholars in the 1980s, and is now used as a broad and inclusive term, which is deliberately ambiguous and open in meaning. As a distinctively English term, queer is untranslatable in other languages. (http://genderqueerid.com/what-is-gq)

Rainbow – a symbol, most widely used as a flag, to visually bring together LGBT and queer identities in representation and activism. Although its usage is now worldwide, it originated in San Francisco, California, in 1978. The choice and number of colours in the flag have undergone numerous variations across time and places, to include other identities and values, though its most common version consists of six horizontal stripes: red, orange, yellow, green, blue, and violet.

References

Puar, Jasbir. 2011. 'Citation and Censorship: The Politics of Talking About the Sexual Politics of Israel' *Feminist Legal Studies*, 19:133.

Rahman, Momin. 2014. *Homosexualities, Muslim cultures and modernity*. Basingstoke, UK: Springer.

Stern, Jean. 2017. *Mirage Gay a Tel Aviv*. Libertalia.

Note on Indexing

Our publications do not feature indexes. If you are reading this book in paperback and want to find a particular word or phrase you can do so by downloading a free PDF version of this book from the E-International Relations website.

View the e-book in any standard PDF reader such as Adobe Acrobat Reader (pc) or Preview (mac) and enter your search terms in the search box. You can then navigate through the search results and find what you are looking for. In practice, this method can prove much more targeted and effective than consulting an index.

If you are using apps (or devices) to read our e-books, you should also find word search functionality in those.

You can find all of our e-books at: http://www.e-ir.info/publications

www.ingramcontent.com/pod-product-compliance
Lightning Source LLC
Chambersburg PA
CBHW030252030426
42336CB00009B/353